This Book Belongs to

Christmas

Book 4

Content and Artwork by **Gooseberry Patch Company**

LEISURE ARTS
Vice President and Editor-in-Chief: Sandra Graham Case
Executive Director of Publications: Cheryl Nodine Gunnells
Director of Designer Relations: Debra Nettles
Publications Director: Kristine Anderson Mertes
Design Director: Cyndi Hansen
Editorial Director: Susan Frantz Wiles
Photography Director: Lori Ringwood Dimond
Art Operations Director: Jeff Curtis
Licensed Product Coordinator: Lisa Truxton Curton

EDITORIAL STAFF

EDITORIAL
Managing Editor: Alan Caudle
Senior Editor: Linda L. Garner

TECHNICAL
Managing Editor: Leslie Schick Gorrell
Book Coordinator and Senior Technical Writer:
    Theresa Hicks Young
Technical Writers: Jean W. Lewis and Kimberly J. Smith

FOODS
Foods Editor: Celia Fahr Harkey, R.D.
Assistant Foods Editor: Jane Kenner Prather
Technical Assistant: Judy Millard

OXMOOR HOUSE
Editor-in-Chief: Nancy Fitzpatrick Wyatt
Executive Editor: Susan Carlisle Payne
Editor: Kelly Hooper Troiano
Photographers: Brit Huckabay and William Dickey
Stylist: Ashley J. Wyatt
Test Kitchen Director: Elizabeth Tyler Luckett
Test Kitchen Assistant Director: Julie Christopher
Recipe Editor: Gayle Hays Sadler
Test Kitchen Staff: Jennifer A. Cofield; Gretchen Feldtman, R.D.;
    David Gallent; Ana Price Kelly; Kathleen Royal Phillips and
    Jan A. Smith
Contributing Stylist: Connie Formby

DESIGN

Lead Designer: Diana Sanders Cates
Designers: Polly Tullis Browning, Cherece Athy,
    Peggy Elliott Cunningham, Anne Pulliam Stocks,
    Linda Diehl Tiano and Becky Werle
Craft Assistant: Lucy Beaudry

ART
Art Director: Mark Hawkins
Senior Production Artist: Mark Potter
Production Artists: Karen Allbright, Elaine Barry and Faith Lloyd
Staff Photographer: Russell Ganser
Staff Photography Stylists: Janna Laughlin and Cassie Newsome
Publishing Systems Administrator: Becky Riddle
Publishing Systems Assistants: Myra S. Means and
    Chris Wertenberger

PROMOTIONS
Associate Editor: Steven M. Cooper
Designer: Dale Rowett
Graphic Artist: Deborah Kelly

BUSINESS STAFF
Publisher: Rick Barton
Vice President, Finance: Tom Siebenmorgen
Director of Corporate Planning and Development:
    Laticia Mull Cornett
Vice President, Retail Marketing: Bob Humphrey
Vice President, Sales: Ray Shelgosh
Vice President, National Accounts: Pam Stebbins
Director of Sales and Services: Margaret Reinold
Vice President, Operations: Jim Dittrich
Comptroller, Operations: Rob Thieme
Retail Customer Service Managers: Sharon Hall and Stan Raynor
Print Production Manager: Fred F. Pruss

Library of Congress Catalog Number 99-71586
Hardcover ISBN 1-57486-253-7
Softcover ISBN 1-57486-254-5

10 9 8 7 6 5 4 3 2 1

Goose berry Patch®

Christmas

Book 4

A LEISURE ARTS PUBLICATION

Christmas

Gooseberry Patch

To our Gooseberry Patch family…wishing you jolly holidays & magical memories!

How Did Gooseberry Patch Get Started?

You may know the story of Gooseberry Patch...the tale of two country friends who decided one day over the backyard fence to try their hands at the mail order business. Started in JoAnn's kitchen back in 1984, Vickie & JoAnn's dream of a "Country Store in Your Mailbox" has grown and grown to a 96-page catalog with over 400 products, including cookie cutters, Santas, snowmen, gift baskets, angels and our very own line of cookbooks! What an adventure for two country friends!

Through our catalogs and books, Gooseberry Patch has met country friends from all over the world. While sharing letters and phone calls, we found that our friends love to cook, decorate, garden and craft. We've created Kate, Holly & Mary Elizabeth to represent these devoted friends who live and love the country lifestyle the way we do. They're just like you & me... they're our "Country Friends®!"

Your friends at Gooseberry Patch

Mary Elizabeth ★ Holly ★ Kate ★ Spot

Contents

SHARING
the MERRY CHRISTMAS SPIRIT 56

Yummy Gifts
from the
KITCHEN 72

Festive Feasting
......86

Keeping Family Traditions

What is Christmas to you? For us, it's the joy of gathering family to celebrate with traditions both old and new, remembering holidays past and, best of all, sharing favorite goodies and recipes! We have lots of ideas to help you create special moments, like a fun-filled family slumber party around the tree, acting out the timeless Nativity story and preserving Grandmother's precious handwritten recipes. Set aside a few moments to yourself and browse through the following pages to find the ideas you like best!

Create a family cookbook that will be treasured as it's passed down. Gather favorite recipes in an album covered with vintage fabric and be sure to tuck in some family photos and handwritten recipe cards. For a heartfelt touch, add snippets from Grandma's kitchen linens or doilies if you have them. Instructions are on page 120.

Taste This Recipe and
~~You'll Really~~

cooking: 5 hr Stew
the kitchen of: M. Cloutier

dry stew
tbl. sugar
tbsp. tapioca
tsp. salt
slice bread (torn in pieces)
1 cup diced celery
6 karots, sliced lengthwise
3 onions, quartered
4 potatoes, sliced lengthwise
2 cups canned
tomatoes juice + puree

Mary

Apple Pie

and dice 4 cups apples
Add 2 cups sugar and let stand.
Beat 2 egg whites stiff add yokes
and beat again. Add 1 cup oil ard
mix well. Combine apple mixture
mixture to egg ard add other
2½ cups flour, 2 tsp. cin
2 tsp. soda, 1 tsp salt
2 tsp. mix and bak

**Aunt Mary's
Famous Apple Pie**

they come out of the oven, onto either a piece
of waxed paper of directly onto the dessert
plates themselves.
    She very carefully explained that if you
these set even a few seconds while you ar
that phone they will break. 'Tis true
believe it but made her taste one

Fruit Salad
Dressing
½ cup sour cream
2 tsp honey
1 tsp orange

Chocolate Upside Down Cake

1st Grease pan, sprinkle nuts on bottom
2nd 3 tablespoons cocoa
1 cup flour
¾ cup sugar
1½ teaspoons baking powder
¼ teaspoons salt
        mix together
add 2 tablespoons melted butter
½ cup of milk

GRANDMA MARTIN'S BEST LO
Chocolate Cake and Fruit Salad

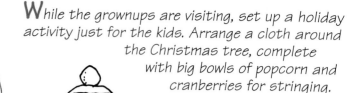

Enjoy a family slumber party! Set up sleeping bags around the tree, have lots of tasty snacks and watch a favorite holiday movie. Before falling asleep, read a Christmas storybook with only the tree lights on.

Let the kids decorate their rooms...a small live or artificial tree, twinkling lights around the windows and mistletoe in the doorway!

If you're lucky enough to enjoy lots of that sparkly white stuff in the winter, take time to play in the snow. Help your kids build a snow fort by packing wet snow into cardboard boxes. Sprinkle the snow with water to form a frozen block, then turn the box upside-down to empty. Stack the snow blocks like bricks to build a wall, a fort or even a castle!

Keep a camera handy during the holidays... snap pictures of kids with cookie faces, rosy cheeks and happy smiles!

Your child can make an Advent chain. Help him or her glue together a paper chain with 25 links, alternating red and green construction paper. Each day, beginning December 1st, tear off one link. Attach this little poem to the top of the chain:
"December 1st to Christmas is the longest time of year,
Seems as though old Santa never will appear.
How many days to Christmas? It's mighty hard to count,
So this little chain will tell you just the right amount."

Take the family ice skating...lots of laughter, guaranteed!

Make a personalized basket for each child and load it up with lots of gifts. Instructions are on page 120.

While the grownups are visiting, set up a holiday activity just for the kids. Arrange a cloth around the Christmas tree, complete with big bowls of popcorn and cranberries for stringing.

For older kids, have plenty of construction paper, white glue, scissors, glitter, sequins, markers and scraps of fabric for making garlands, snowflakes and ornaments. Be sure to hang on to all those sweet, humble ornaments your children make through the years. They become more precious as time goes by!

My 20-year-old daughter has always shared Christmas Eve with the reindeer. As a child, before going to bed, she put out special cookies and hot cocoa for Santa, but she felt sorry for the reindeer. So we went to the kitchen and cut up fresh carrots and celery and she scattered them about the front yard, then went to bed with a sigh of relief. Thanks to her, the reindeer would not go hungry that busy night.

— Jan Kouzes

Help your children keep the spirit of Christmas... they can shovel a driveway or sidewalk for a neighbor, baby-sit for a busy mom or deliver goodies to a secret pal. Your children will learn that they benefit more than the receivers.

Right next to your coziest chair...fill a basket with favorite Christmas books for all age levels. Be sure to have a warm quilt for snuggling under and a table nearby for steamy cups of cocoa. Toss in some adults and kids for a great Christmas memory!

Rolls of Ribbon, tape & tags... Christmas Wrap and Shopping Bags!

☆

Let your kids help with the gift wrapping!

Kids will love having a Christmasy chair of their very own! Simply paint on happy snowmen and colorful light bulbs. Instructions begin on page 120.

Make a tree skirt to remember your children or grandchildren. Choose a plain fabric and put a fringe or border on to your liking. With chalk, trace each child's handprint. Have the mother or you embroider the hand, child's name and year. You can add to this forever!

— Pauline Williams
Hendersonville, TN

We act out the Christmas story on Christmas Eve. Older children can narrate, younger ones can act. We use a stick horse for the donkey, towels for the shepherds' heads, paper crowns for the Wise Men and gold garland for angel halos. It is so much fun, and it makes a great video.

— Gale Wightman

On cold mornings around the holidays, put green food coloring in oatmeal for your children and grandchildren. Cinnamon sprinkled on top adds a festive touch.

— Jackie Stephens

This year, run your household on "holiday time" with a specially decorated clock! Instructions for our decoupaged timepiece can be found on page 121.

Handmade labels give extra-special appeal to jars of homemade goodies. For the instructions, turn to page 121.

A loving gift for your child straight from the heart…assemble a recipe box with all of Grandma's and Mom's family recipes. Add new recipes each year, along with funny little notes and sayings. A warm, wonderful gift to grow right along with your child…truly a box full of memories!

If you have treasured handwritten recipes, photocopy them to share with family. It's heartwarming to see your favorites in Grandma's handwriting.

Old-fashioned glass canning jars are perfect for holding gifts from your kitchen! Fill them with dry mixes like homemade cocoa or your favorite layered cookie mix. You can also give jars filled with hearty homemade soup or friendship bread starter.

Paint or stencil a winter scene on your glass canning jar before you fill it! Dip a sponge into paint, blot off the excess and decorate your jar. When the paint's dry, coat the jar with a sealer.

When you give cookies as gifts, be sure to include the recipe. You can make your own recipe cards: use pinking shears to cut small hearts from fabric and glue them onto lined note cards. Tie the cards to your gifts with jute string for a country touch.

Great stocking-stuffers for a cook: unusual cookbooks, kitchen towels, spices and recipe cards.

Share favorite recipes with a dear friend…such a simple gift will mean a great deal.

Wrap your homemade canned preserves or salsa in festive tissue or cellophane bags tied with ribbons or raffia. Set them in a basket by the door and give to guests as they leave, or keep them for that unexpected moment when a gift is needed. They make a pretty decoration, too!

Include a favorite holiday recipe with your Christmas cards. Friends and family will love trying out your "tastes of Christmas!"

Decoupage color copies of family photos from past Christmases on a clay pot. Plant a poinsettia inside for a great gift, or use the decorated pot as a pencil cup on your desk.

Create a Christmas keepsake album...add snippets of wrapping paper, holiday photos, special cards and heartfelt handwritten notes or letters.

Always remember during Christmas that a homemade gift from the heart means more to someone than a present bought from the store. Last year's gift was one of the best I could have ever given my grandma. Going through her photo albums, I came across old pictures of her family and borrowed them. I then bought a picture frame, the kind with the different-shaped openings, and beautifully arranged the pictures of her family. When my grandma unwrapped my gift she was pleasantly surprised to have received such a thoughtful gift made from the heart.

— Crystal Parker
Worthington, OH

"Other things may change us, but we start and end with family."

— Anthony Brandt

Jazz up an old paper lampshade with a handful of holiday photos...use adhesive and black photo corners to affix them.

Buttoned-up photo board: Buy a wooden-framed cork bulletin board and paint the frame red or green; then hot glue Christmasy buttons all the way around. You may want to add other tiny trinkets to the button mix, too...try charms, dime-store gems and old costume jewelry, marbles or teensy toys for a delightful look. Don't forget to decorate your push pins...glue buttons to flat-top metal tacks for a fun way to pin up holiday photos and cards!

Create a collage to remember special celebrations and get-togethers! Glue on color copies of photographs, Christmas cards and postcards, gift tags, bits of wrapping paper or ribbon, copies of handwritten recipes, menus or anything that's a sweet reminder of that special occasion.

As family and friends come over during the holidays, take an instant snapshot of them around the tree, table, or outside in the snow. Have some pretty metallic or designer paper on hand and mount the snapshot onto the paper. Trim the edges of mounting paper with pinking shears. Have your guests decorate the edges with sequins, stickers, dried berries or flowers, then use colorful markers to write in the date and occasion at the bottom of the picture (in the white rectangular space). Your guests now have a personalized, dated ornament to take home with them. Especially fun for the kids.

— Deena Funk

Take lots of pictures, hold hands, sing, laugh and make every Christmas one to remember.

"Memories are like keepsakes... always to be treasured."

— Unknown

Here's a neat way to display treasured holiday photos and cards...spread them out on a tabletop or trunk lid! Don't forget to cover them with a piece of glass cut to fit so they'll be protected.

For those relatives far away at holiday time, make a videotape of your family in front of the Christmas tree, opening the gifts those relatives sent. Include personal messages and then send a copy of the tape to these special people.

— Susan Thompson

Memory is the treasury and guardian of all things.
— CICERO —

What a clever way to display your "family tree!" We used an old measuring cup trimmed with rick-rack and buttons to hold the coiled wire "branches." The instructions are on page 121.

When older family members, such as grandparents or great aunts and uncles, are visiting for the holidays, keep a guest book handy and ask them to write a page or two of their favorite memories as a child. What was Christmas like in their home? Can they recall their favorite Christmas? Perhaps they could write their favorite recipe for a holiday treat in the book. Your memory book can be packed away each year with the Christmas ornaments and placed out on the coffee table the next year. It's fun to read and recall best memories of those loved ones and their good old days.

— Juanita Williams
Jacksonville, OR

Decking the Halls

Christmas is here again...it's time to deck the halls and trim the tree! Let the Country Friends® help you spread cheer all through the house: Mary Elizabeth has already made 12 dozen mitten ornaments for her tree, and Holly is busy collecting evergreen boughs and sprigs to make wreaths and garlands. Kate's a little behind...she's planning to start decorating by December 24th at the very latest!

Frosty fun abounds with these snowy sap buckets! Just paint, apply a colorful picture and add lots of textured snow. Fill buckets with greenery and pine cones, or load them up with goodies and gifts! See page 121 for complete instructions.

A Homespun Welcome Hi

More fun with sap buckets…paint a small one to hang on the front door or add one of our illustrations and a sprinkling of stars. If you can't find sap buckets, pails from the hardware store will work just fine.

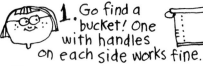

DO-IT-YOURSELF SAP BUCKET Door Decoration!

1. Go find a bucket! One with handles on each side works fine.

2. Now remove the bottom of the bucket. Use pliers or a hammer and screwdriver to pop it right out.

3. Okay, "PINCH" the bucket at the bottom to flatten it. The handles should be on the sides and the bottom pinched shut. Use pliers to turn up the bottom of the bucket ~ it will look kind of like this ⟶ from the side.

4. Now make a pretty bow from 1½ yards of ribbon. Leave the "streamers" fairly long and tie to the bucket handles. Now you've made the hanger!

5. Line your bucket with heavy plastic… fill the bucket with wet Oasis®…then add fresh greenery. Neat!

A blue spatterware bucket looks great filled with bright red apples, or fill a red sugar bucket with green Granny Smith apples.

Spray paint an empty coffee can with gold paint, tie it up with a gold ribbon and fill with fresh holly branches and fragrant greenery.

18

SAP BUCKET ORNAMENTS

Paint a small sap bucket a Christmasy color; lightly sand the bucket to remove some of the paint down to the metal. Make a color copy of your favorite image from page 135; cut it out and glue it to the bucket…you can use a sticker instead if you'd like. Use a gold paint pen to draw tiny stars around the image, then use a black marker to outline the stars and add clusters of dots around them.

If you want to add a handle, use an awl to punch a hole in each side of the bucket. Thread the ends of a length of heavy-duty wire through the holes and bend them to secure.

A painted pail or sap bucket is perfect for holding everything you'll need to start a cozy fire on a chilly winter night! Lots of pine cones, fatwood sticks, fireplace matches, sprigs of dried herbs and twigs can be tucked inside.

19

If you have urns on your porch, fill them with greenery, then set a pineapple in the middle...a very old-fashioned welcome symbol!

Frost the glass panes in an old wooden window frame with snow spray and then write fun messages in the "snow." Hang it on your porch to greet guests!

A basket of greenery on the seat of an old rocking chair, a sled leaning against the rail and a pint-size evergreen in a child's red wagon...a pretty winter welcome for your porch!

t is easier to go on and on,
DREADFUL happens.

— Laura Ingalls
Wilder

CHRISTMAS LIGHTS WELCOME MAT

A simple sponge-painted mat is a bright idea to welcome friends into your home. Trace the letter and light patterns, page 135, onto tracing paper. Use the patterns to cut shapes from compressed craft sponges, then use the sponges to paint a sisal mat. "String" the lights together with a painted-on electric cord and let them dry.

Tie a spray of greenery and some wooly mittens to a pair of crossed snow shoes or wooden skis, then set them by the front door to celebrate winter!

Naturally Festive

Create a beautiful setting with nature's bounty...it's easy! Just gather lush evergreens, scarlet berries, rustic pine cones and raffia, and you're ready to begin.

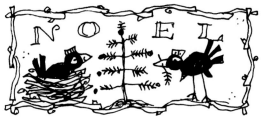

A small potted cedar tree is just right for tucking into a corner to bring Christmas cheer! Trim it with mini berry wreaths, tiny birds' nests and other naturals; see page 121 for the instructions. After the holidays, it can be planted outside as a sweet reminder of the season. Dress a window with sprays of greenery and cedar boughs tied with raffia...so beautiful and oh, so simple!

A moss wreath with fragrant eucalyptus welcomes visitors with seasonal cheer…but why stop at the door? Hang berry-bright miniature grapevine wreaths on cabinet doors or in your windows, too!

An old European custom: Prickly holly in the house at Christmas meant that the husband would rule during the coming year; smooth holly meant that the wife would rule.

Add a sweet holiday fragrance to your crackling fire…just toss in a handful of dried mint leaves, orange peel or cinnamon sticks!

EUCALYPTUS WREATH

For the base, cut an 18-inch square from a piece of 2-inch thick plastic foam, then cut out a 5-inch square at the center. Cover the top and sides of the base with a thick layer of glue…press sheet moss into the glue. Arrange fresh stems of eucalyptus over the moss and secure in place with floral pins.

MINI WREATHS

For our simple raffia-bow wreath, wrap and glue a small berry garland around a 10" diameter grapevine wreath. Glue sprigs of fresh cedar to the bottom of the wreath, then tie several strands of raffia into a bow and glue to greenery…add a couple of sprigs of red berries.

To make the pepperberry wreath, hot glue bunches of pepperberries to the front of a 10" diameter grapevine wreath. For the hanger, thread the ends of a 14" long piece of 1½" wide ribbon through the top of the wreath…overlap and glue the ends together. Tie a 12" long piece of ribbon into a bow, then glue the knot of the bow to the top of the hanger.

In no time at all, you'll have quick & easy decorations for every door or window in the house.

The herbs of Christmas: chamomile, horehound, lavender, rosemary, thyme and sweet woodruff. Legend has it that Mary hung her wash to dry on lavender and rosemary plants. The swaddling clothes of Baby Jesus gave the scentless lavender plant its wonderful fragrance. It is also said that Mary's cloak changed the white rosemary blossoms to blue. The other herbs are thought to have been mixed with the straw in the manger.

Gilded leaves make beautiful decorations for gift packages, garlands or your Christmas tree. Simply dip leaves into gold or silver paint, or lightly spray with color. Certain leaves have special meanings: aspen stands for imagination, maple for strength and birch for good fortune and new beginnings.

Core several fresh artichokes and allow them to dry out. Spray them with gold paint and let dry. Tuck a votive candle in each and set on your table or mantel for a lovely holiday glow.

GIFT WRAP

To "age" a new terra cotta flowerpot, turn it upside down, rub the outside with buttermilk and place it in a dark closet for about three weeks. It'll look like it's been weathering for years!

Uncoil ropes of wide twisted paper to wrap gifts; tie with raffia and add a few cedar sprigs for a natural touch. Nestle candles in clay pots filled with greenery, moss and berries. We salvaged an old watering can, painted it with crackle medium and planted a tiny cedar tree to trim with eucalyptus, berries and rusted star garland.

Create naturally festive candleholders! Carve out apples and oranges and tuck in votive candles...pretty and fragrant!

CANDLE COLLECTION

Gather every white candle you can find…short and tall pillars, votives, tea lights…all will do. Wire rusty tin stars onto a few candles and wrap rusted craft wire around several more. Snuggle smaller candles, votives and tea lights into painted clay saucers that have been lightly sanded for a gently aged look. Nestle the candles and saucers among boughs of fresh greenery, dried berries, pomegranates and other wintry naturals. But please be sure to keep your holidays safe…never leave burning candles unattended!

A collection of pillar candles is pretty as a table centerpiece. Wrap tall ones with cinnamon sticks, secured with a wide homespun bow. Small chubby ones can be grouped in a stoneware pie plate.

Decorate with lots of candles...tall, fat, short; set tea lights in bowls of coarse salt, or fill an empty fireplace with candles!

All Hearts come Home for Christmas

Even if we're far from home, our hearts remember loved ones at Christmas. Why not show your heartfelt sentiments with cozy decorations? Instructions for the afghan and nostalgic sampler begin on page 121.

Cut felt in the shapes of stars, mittens, stockings or hearts and blanket stitch them in the corner of a flannel blanket…perfect for curling up under on a chilly night!

For your kitchen, trim a little tree with shiny tin and copper heart-shaped cookie cutters. Tie them to the branches with strips of red fabric.

To make a dried cranberry heart, use a fine-gauge wire and a strong craft needle to string the cranberries, then shape the wire into a heart. Top with a piece of homespun tied with some sprigs of pine. Hang on the kitchen wall or above your mantel.

KEY ORNAMENT

Spray a large skeleton key with rust-colored primer and allow to dry. Follow manufacturer's instructions to apply a crackle medium, then a top coat of ivory paint to the key. Thread a 12-inch length of $^5/_8$" wide ribbon through the loop in the key, then tie the ribbon into a bow.

FELT HEART ORNAMENT

- freezer paper
- one ecru and 2 red 7-inch squares of felt
- pinking shears
- small, very sharp scissors
- 12-inches of red grosgrain ribbon
- polyester fiberfill

What's the key to a heartfelt Christmas? Decorations made with love! Whether you're giving these away or keeping a few for yourself, the nostalgic key and heart-shaped ornaments, along with the matching tree skirt and mini cross-stitched sampler, will bring warm and cozy feelings this holiday season. The tree skirt and sampler ornament instructions are on page 122.

1. Trace heart pattern, page 132, onto dull side of freezer paper.

2. Iron pattern, shiny side down, onto one red felt square. Pin the ecru felt to the opposite side of the red felt.

3. For ornament front, with paper side up, sew felt pieces together along drawn lines. Use pinking shears to cut out ecru heart only 1/4" outside outer sewn line. Cutting through ecru felt only, use small scissors to cut out areas in heart between sewn lines. Carefully tear away pattern.

4. With ecru heart on top, pin ornament front to remaining piece of red felt. Using pinking shears, cut out ornament 1/2" larger than ecru heart. For the hanger, fold ribbon in half and pin ends together between felt layers at top of ornament. Leaving an opening for stuffing, sew pieces together 1/4" outside edges of ecru heart. Lightly stuff ornament with fiberfill, then sew opening closed.

Let it

When the weather is chilly, nothing warms us up like the glow of candlelight! Votives are just the right size for scattering throughout the house, and they're even more festive nestled in decorated holders. Instructions for the glittery ones are right here; to make the candleholders shown opposite, turn to page 122.

FROSTED GLOBE CANDLEHOLDERS

- clear self-adhesive paper
- clear globe-shaped candleholders
- paper towels
- spray adhesive
- white iridescent glitter
- desired colors of acrylic paint
- paintbrushes

1. Trace tree and dot or stars patterns, page 157, onto self-adhesive paper for desired number of shapes; cut out shapes. Arrange and adhere shapes to candleholder.

2. Fill candleholder with paper towels to protect from spray adhesive. Apply spray adhesive to candleholder; cover adhesive with glitter. Gently shake off loose glitter; remove paper towels.

3. Remove paper shapes from candleholder; paint shapes as desired, then allow to dry. (More than one coat of paint may be necessary for desired coverage.)

34

Make your own candles! Shop discount stores or thrift shops for inexpensive glasses, little demitasse mugs, dessert goblets and other interesting holders. Melt wax or paraffin in a coffee can placed in boiling water (an electric skillet works well for this)...tint with candle dye or old crayons and add candle fragrance if you like. Warm the glasses with hot water, then fill with wax and cool completely. To add wicks, heat an ice pick over an open flame; carefully poke a hole in the center of the candle, almost all the way through. Insert wick in hole and trim to 3/8" above the top of the candle. Great for special gifts!

Snuggle in

Remember when you were little and couldn't wait for the first snow of the season? It was so much fun bundling up to build a snowman and then snuggling in by the fire afterward to enjoy a cup of chocolatey cocoa! Our oversize mitten "stocking" and pint-size snowman, mitten and star ornaments bring back those childhood memories. Stocking instructions begin on page 39.

SNOWMAN ORNAMENTS

Adorn a tree, wreath or even a window with these frosty snowman ornaments! For each ornament, cut two 4¹/₂" diameter circles from white fabric. Trace the face pattern from page 149 onto tracing paper, then use transfer paper to transfer the design to the center of one of the circles. Paint the face…while it's drying, tear a 1"x8" strip from homespun for the hanger; fold the strip in half to form a loop. Place the circles together with the face to the inside…insert the hanger between the circles with the ends extending slightly at the top. Leaving an opening for turning, sew the circles together. Turn the ornament right-side out, lightly stuff with polyester fiberfill and sew the opening closed.

WOODEN STAR ORNAMENTS

These star ornaments are quick & easy…a perfect project for all the kids to help with, too! Paint both sides of a wooden star cut-out yellow and allow to dry. Use a black marker to draw "stitches" along the edges of the star, then glue a big button to the front. Hot glue stars here and there to add a "twinklie" touch.

MITTEN ORNAMENTS

Using the mitten pattern from page 139 and a 4"x6¹/₂" cuff, follow Steps 1 and 3 from the **Mitten Stocking or Pillows** on page 39 to make each ornament; use clear thread to make a hanging loop on the back of the cuff. Shape a wire "curlique" by wrapping craft wire around a pencil, then stretching it out a little. Hot glue a **Wooden Star Ornament** from this page to the wire and tuck it in the mitten along with fresh greenery.

FABRIC STAR ORNAMENTS

Tear a 1"x8" strip from homespun for the hanger; fold the strip in half to form a loop. Trace the star pattern, page 139, onto tracing paper. Use the pattern to cut two star shapes from fabric and one from batting. Matching right sides, place the star shapes together…insert the hanger between the stars with the ends extending slightly past one point. Layer the batting star on top and pin layers together. Leaving an opening for turning, sew the stars together. Turn the ornament right-side out and sew the opening closed.

Frosty fun abounds when you trim an evergreen wreath with jolly snowman and wooden star ornaments; instructions on page 37. The jumbo mitten pillows will cozy up any corner.

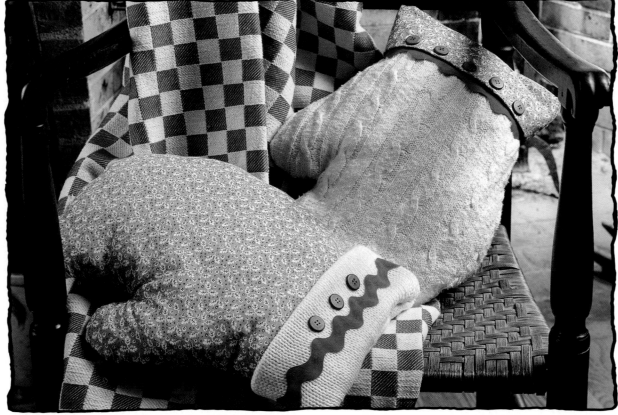

MITTEN STOCKING OR PILLOWS

- unbleached muslin
- tracing paper
- fabric or old sweater
- rick-rack
- assorted buttons
- polyester fiberfill

Use a $1/4$" seam allowance for all sewing unless otherwise indicated. Before cutting shapes from a sweater, fuse a piece of muslin to the wrong side to stabilize the knit.

1. Enlarge the mitten pattern pieces from page 140 by 200%, then follow *Making Patterns*, page 130, to make a pattern for your pillow or stocking. Use pattern to cut two (one in reverse) mitten shapes. Matching right sides and leaving the top open, sew the mitten pieces together; turn right-side out.

2. For the hanger on the stocking, cut a $1^1/2$"x6" strip of fabric. Matching right sides, press strip in half lengthwise; sew long edges together. Turn hanger right-side out and fold in half. Matching ends of hanger with the top edge of the mitten, baste hanger in mitten at the seam.

3. For the cuff, measure width of mitten at top edge; cut an $8^1/2$" wide strip from fabric or sweater the determined measurement. Matching right sides, sew the ends together. Matching wrong sides and raw edges, fold the cuff in half.

Place the cuff inside the mitten, matching the raw edges with the top edge of the mitten. Sew around the edge and fold the cuff to the outside of the mitten.

4. Sew rick-rack and buttons on the mitten as desired.

5. For pillows, stuff with fiberfill and sew opening closed.

Don't forget to have lots of fluffy pillows on hand for holiday visitors…and little ones who want to snuggle! Overnight guests will feel extra-special if you dress their bed in cheery red and green flannel sheets and add a cozy quilt, too.

Continue the snowy theme with a "life-size" pillow; instructions on page 122. Trim a basket with one of the mitten ornaments and fill it with gifts, fresh greenery or firestarters. The friendly snowman and fabric star ornaments look great hung in the window, too! Ornament instructions on page 37.

Put the Christmas tree lights on a timer switch. That way, you're not crawling over gifts Christmas Eve or morning to get the lights plugged in.

A very lovely Christmas sharing idea for a group of children is to make a "Mitten Christmas Tree" from cardboard and attach it to a wall. Each child in the group is asked to bring in a new pair of mittens from home to decorate the tree. Before Christmas arrives, the mittens are taken down by the children and delivered to a specific shelter for children and adults. The children take great pleasure seeing their decorations are going to help so many people who might experience cold hands and fingers during the upcoming months.

— Jan Kouzes

Attract all kinds of birds to your snowman: Before adding his hat, sprinkle birdseed on the brim. Use dried apples and raisins for his eyes and mouth, and hollow out orange halves for buttons.

Jolly Old St. Nicholas

*Santa Claus, Father Christmas,
St. Nicholas…no matter what we
call him, the very mention of his name
brings a thrill of anticipation to young
and old alike. He looks especially
sweet stitched in redwork embroidery
on our patchwork wall hanging.
Instructions are on page 123.*

My favorite Christmas tradition was celebrating St. Nicholas Day, which falls on December 6th. On the night of the 5th, we'd hang our stockings up and go to bed. In the morning, we'd find tangerines, a St. Nick cookie and a piece of paper. The paper held a rhyme that was a clue to where our gifts were hidden. We'd find our gifts from St. Nick and tear open the wrappings. I can still "smell" those mornings…the tangerine peel, the nutmeg from the cookie and the excitement of opening the packages. Mom was smart, because December 25th seems a lifetime away when Thanksgiving is past, so having a little treat earlier helped with the anticipation and excitement of waiting.

— Teresa Labat
Castro Valley, CA

"Not believe in Santa Claus? You might as well not believe in fairies."

— Frances P. Church

Joy ~ wishes ~ blessings ~ love

Winter Windows

Don't forget to dress your windows in holiday finery! Try hanging frosted "gingerbread cookies" or a vintage bottle filled with berries, or create a faux stained glass pattern.

FROSTED JAR

Adhere star-shaped stickers to a clean jar and spray the jar with frosted glass finish. Allow the jar to dry, then remove the stickers. Wrap heavy-duty craft wire around the neck of the jar and twist ends together to secure...hook and twist the ends of a long length of wire at each side of jar under the first wire to form a handle. Soak honeysuckle vines in water until pliable. Twist vines around handle as desired; glue ends to secure.

CHRISTMAS STAINED GLASS WINDOW

This is so easy that Mary Elizabeth wants to do all the windows in her house! Use silver leading to draw a border of wide stripes across the top of a "gently-weathered" window...draw several round ornaments with holly leaves "hanging" from the border. Use your favorite Christmas colors of acrylic glass paints to paint the stripes, ornaments and leaves...paint the remaining glass clear.

CHRISTMAS "COOKIE" ORNAMENTS

These cookies look good enough to eat, but they're made from copper-colored sculpting clay! Use Christmasy cookie cutters to cut shapes from clay just as if you were making real cookies (don't use any of your good kitchen tools for this), then bake your cookies until golden. For the "icing", mix $\frac{1}{2}$-part water with one part textured snow medium; fill a cake decorating bag with the icing, then freehand designs onto your gingerbread creations. Glue a big red button to the front of each ornament and the ends of a length of rickrack to the back for a hanger.

Have a white Christmas even without the snow! Use a damp sponge to apply white water-soluble paint to the bottom corners of windowpanes using pre-cut holiday stencils or create your own designs with cookie cutters and construction paper. Paper doilies make wonderful intricate snowflake designs, too. Try decorating an old wooden window frame; attach hooks on the top and hang it on your porch to greet guests!

Hang this little angel in a sunny window to keep watch over your holiday preparations. And you'll want to be on your best behavior…you never know when Santa will come peeking at the window! Instructions for the painted window are on page 123.

ANGEL SUN CATCHER

Use a fine-point marker to trace the angel pattern, page 145, onto the front of a piece of clear rigid plastic. Crumple, then smooth a piece of white tissue paper large enough to cover your pattern. Apply a thin layer of glue to the back of the plastic piece, then smooth tissue paper onto glue and allow to dry. Use black leading to draw over marker lines on front of sun catcher; allow to dry. Cut out the sun catcher just outside the leading lines. Mix equal parts of water and paint. Use the mixture to paint tissue paper side of the sun catcher; allow to dry. Use a pushpin to make a small hole at the top of the sun catcher; thread a length of nylon thread through hole and tie ends together for a hanger.

Decorate your bay window to look like a toy store window! Bring out a variety of stuffed animals, wrapped packages, festive decorations, a train set, dolls or even a tiny decorated tree!

— Balynda Elkins
Paulding, OH

What child can resist the appeal of gingerbread decorations trimmed with icing and candies? For a fun variation, use your cookie cutters to make whimsical animal "pull toys." You'll find easy how-to's on page 123.

At Christmastime, I put together gingerbread families for all my grandchildren. I have a Mama, Papa, sister and brothers, along with pet bears or dogs, and each one has a tiny red satin ribbon tied around its neck. I pack these "families" in Christmas tins or colorful small paper bags. Who says children shouldn't play with their food?

— Tamara Gruber
Houston, TX

Treats

About a week before Christmas, when school is out, we have a cookie decorating party. Both of my children, now 12 and 14, invite three or four friends. Using a butter cookie recipe and lots of different Christmas cookie cutters, we bake about 2 dozen cookies per person. We also decorate and personalize a plain, inexpensive apron for each guest. For the cookies, we buy **tons** of sprinkles, tubes of icing, and colored sparkles. The kids get busy creating, and lots of munching goes on! Milk and hot cider are served, and each guest leaves with a large red or green plastic plate filled with cookies. It's always a hit!

— Patricia Donza
Greenwich, CT

Vintage Delights

Old-time postcards, glass ornaments, bottle brush trees…for collectors, searching for vintage Christmas finds at flea markets and yard sales is a year 'round delight. Try framing an old-fashioned card with tinsel, or place antique tree toppers in glass candlesticks of varying heights and arrange with greenery and ribbon for a centerpiece.

GREETING CARD DECORATION

Vintage greeting and postcards bring a sweet, old-fashioned feel to holiday decorations. Tuck them in a basket, nestle some among the greenery on a mantel or use color copies to make this holiday greeting…it's easy. Enlarge card on a photocopier to the desired size, then glue the card to a piece of foam core board. Trim to the same size as card, then glue garland along the edges for a twinklie eye-catcher. Tie a length of ribbon into a bow with really long streamers; glue the mounted card to the streamers and notch the ends. Hang on a door knob, pegrack or in a window to welcome guests.

Remember the old-fashioned lights on Grandma's tree? This year, use lots of colorful, vintage-style lights to capture those feelings of Christmases past.

A nostalgic Christmas "tree"…stack glass cake stands, arrange your favorite glass ornaments and fill in with fresh greenery. Whiteware cups and pots provide the perfect setting for a collection of bottle brush trees.

BOTTLE BRUSH TREES

Reminiscent of snow dusted branches, these frosty bottle brush trees bring the season inside. Fill whiteware containers with floral foam, then cover the foam with batting. "Plant" your tree and apply tiny bits of snow medium for "new-fallen" snow. Glue on miniature ornaments or pearls for extra sparkle.

Fill an old apothecary jar or hurricane shade with rosehips, cranberries, vintage Christmas balls or cinnamon sticks. Surrounded with greenery, it makes a festive centerpiece.

The More the Merrier!

Use color copies of old-fashioned postcards to make the prettiest gift tags, or use several to transform a stack of suitcases…it's oh-so-simple!

VINTAGE GIFT TAG

Make one of these quick & easy gift tags for everyone on your gift-giving list. Simply make a reduced color copy of a copyright-free vintage card on card stock, then cut out. Glue the card onto another piece of card stock and trim the edges with decorative-edge craft scissors…repeat for the back border.

SHARING
the MERRY CHRISTMAS SPIRIT

From Holly ★

♥love, mary elizabeth

To ♥Frosty ♥ kate

Y̲ou don't have to spend a lot of money to spread Christmas cheer! Even the simplest offering can be unforgettable when it's crafted and given with love. Make this year extra-special with one-of-a-kind gifts...goodie baskets tailored to the recipient's interests, custom-designed slippers or caps, a cuddly snowman doll and even stockings for the family pets!

I'm "SEW" glad we're Friends!

For gifts that can't be beat, pack decorated baskets with lots of little treats...choose themes that you know the recipients will enjoy. Instructions for the baskets shown here begin on page 124.

Star Pupil

Star Pupil

Emily from Holly

GOODIES ★TO★ GO

A gift basket doesn't have to begin with a basket! Find an old-time wire milk bottle carrier…fill milk bottles or canning jars with a variety of candies, or surprise a friend who loves to garden with a colorfully painted pot packed with gardening goodies.

GIFT-FILLED MILK BOTTLES

- glass quart-size milk bottles
- craft knife and cutting mat
- poster board
- permanent fine-point markers
- colored pencils
- craft glue
- photocopy of the tag design on page 156 on white card stock
- red card stock
- decorative-edge craft scissors

Allow glue to dry after each application.

1. For each milk cap, measure inside diameter of the bottle opening; cut two circles from poster board the determined measurement. Cut a small "U" shape at the center of one circle and bend up for a pull tab. Use markers and colored pencils to draw desired words or designs (we drew green holly leaves and red berries) on tab circle. Glue the circles together and insert in filled bottle.

2. Cut out tag along lines; use colored pencils to color design. Glue tag to red card stock; use craft scissors to trim card stock 1/4" outside tag edges.

GARDEN GIFT POT

- spray primer
- red acrylic spray paint
- 6" tall clay pot
- tracing paper
- compressed craft sponge
- transfer paper
- yellow, white and green acrylic paint
- liner paintbrush
- yellow paint pen
- clear acrylic spray sealer
- white and red card stock
- craft glue stick
- hole punch
- black permanent fine-point marker
- lunch-size paper bags
- green raffia

Allow paint and sealer to dry after each application.

1. Apply primer, then 2 coats of red paint to entire pot.

2. Trace the star and verse patterns, page 157, onto tracing paper. Use the star pattern to cut a star shape from sponge. Use transfer paper to transfer the verse onto the front of the pot.

3. *Sponge Paint*, page 130, yellow stars around the rim of the pot; paint vertical white lines between the stars. Use the paint pen to trace over the verse and the end of the paintbrush handle to paint green dots randomly on pot.

4. Apply two coats of sealer to pot.

5. For each tag, cut a 1³/₄"x2¹/₄" piece of white card stock. Glue tag to red card stock, then trim to ¹/₄" from edges of tag; punch a hole in one corner. *Sponge Paint* yellow stars on tag, then use marker to write message at center of tag. Fill paper bags with desired garden items and tie closed with raffia. Thread tag onto raffia and tie into a bow. Fill pot with bags and other items for your favorite gardener.

*O*ther gift basket ideas: For a book lover, fill a book bag with a stack of newly released paperbacks, a bookmark, personalized bookplates and a book light. For a golfer, begin with a golf hat, turned upside down...fill it up with colorful tees and golf balls. Attach a little canary on the brim of the hat (a birdie...get it?). For the fishing fanatic on your list, mount a small branch on a block of pine so it looks like a miniature tree, then hang with new fishing lures and bobbers. For a sports buff...tape tickets for a college game or minor league event to a bottle of sports drink; drop inside a team-colored tube sock and tie closed with bright streamers.

OH BOY! SANTA CLAUS IS COMING!

Whether they're tiny and hanging on the tree or full-size and filled to the brim with goodies, these appliquéd stockings are sure to be a hit! Instructions for making the penny rug-style designs are on page 124.

Little Things mean A lot!

Great stocking stuffers: tin cookie cutters, Mom's recipes, bookmarks, a diary, homemade candies, vintage charms, scented votive candles, a snowman pin, a favorite snapshot in a tiny frame, red woolly mittens, seeds for spring, a little flag and movie tickets.

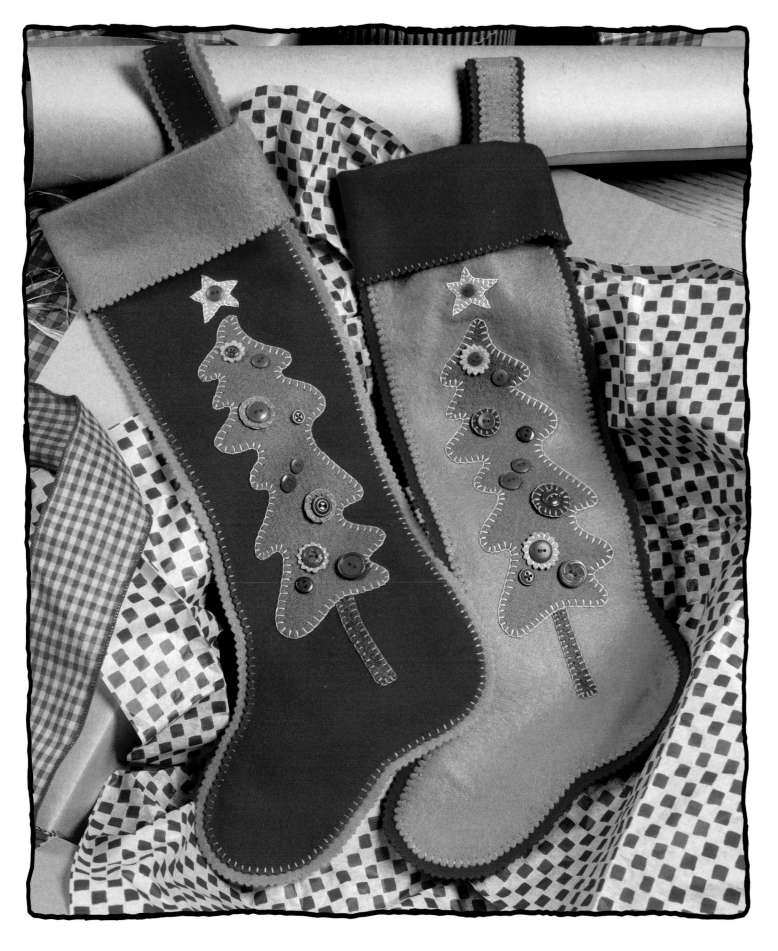

Countdown to CHRISTMAS

Need to make a bunch of little gifts? You can whip up fancy paper wraps for scented votives in no time, or try your hand at soap-making…it's easier than you think! The loaf-like loofah soap can be sliced to make several "scrubbers," the little muffin-tin soaps are scented with lavender and the Christmas tree bars are packaged in festive wrappers.

GUEST GIFT VOTIVES

For each candle wrap, copy the triangle pattern, page 148, onto card stock. Use decorative-edge craft scissors to cut out the triangle. Using a star-shaped stamp and gold and yellow ink, stamp stars randomly on the outside of the triangle…use a brown marker to make lots of dots around the stars and to write a message on one flap. Fold the flaps along the dotted lines. Glue a 6-inch length of $^{3}/_{8}$" wide ribbon from fold to point on inside of each flap. Place a votive candle at the center of the wrap, thread a jingle bell onto the ribbons and tie ribbons into a bow to secure. Place in a basket by the door to give to guests on their way home!

SIMPLE SOAPS

There are lots of soap-making supplies available in the craft stores. Follow the manufacturer's instructions to melt the soaps and add desired colors. When making soaps, be sure to use old pans or tins that you no longer use for baking.

Loofah Soaps

Spray a metal loaf pan with candle mold release. Place one large or 2 small loofah sponges in the pan. Pour glycerin soap into the pan over the loofah sponges and let harden. (Soap should cover about half of the height of the sponges.) Remove loofah from pan, then use a sharp knife to cut into slices. Place each slice into a cellophane bag and tie closed with raffia.

Muffin-Tin Soap

Spray a muffin tin with candle mold release. Add pieces of dried lavender to melted, white soap, then pour the soap into the tin. Allow soap to harden, remove from tin, place each soap in a clear cellophane bag and tie closed with raffia.

Tree Soaps

Ok, these are a little bit harder, but not too bad. For the tree, find a tree-shaped rubber stamp a little smaller than your soap mold. Remove the stamp from the wooden block and place in the mold...the side that was attached to the block should be down. Spray the mold and stamp with candle mold release. Now, fill the tree shape in the stamp with green glycerin soap and let it harden. Next, fill the mold with white soap and allow to harden. Remove the soap from the mold and carefully peel the stamp from the soap. Repeat to make as many soaps as you need. Wrap the soap in clear plastic wrap. Use decorative-edge craft scissors to cut a narrow strip of red paper to wrap around the soap. Overlapping the ends at the back, glue a strip of handmade paper, then the red strip around the soap. Use rubber cement to reattach the stamp to the wooden block, then stamp a tree on card stock for the tag. Paint the tree and let it dry. Leaving a narrow border, cut out the tag and punch a hole near the top. Knot several strands of raffia around the soap, then tie on the tag.

Hand-made Holidays

It's the little touches that make the season unforgettable…hand-painted goblets for holiday toasts, simple patchwork coasters or a festive needlepoint pillow for a friend.

PAINTED CHRISTMAS GOBLET

Turn an ordinary piece of stemmed glassware into a holiday favorite…just remember to let the paint dry between applications. Using acrylic paint for glass, paint two red parallel lines around the goblet, then paint the stem and base red. Paint green holly leaves around the bottom of the stem and between the lines; use the end of the paintbrush handle to add a few red berries to the leaves between the lines and to paint white dots here and there on the goblet. So easy, you could make an entire set of these for that special time of year.

PATCHWORK COASTER

Cut one 6"x7" piece each from felt and paper-backed fusible web; fuse web to felt for the coaster backing; remove paper backing. Cut a 5-sided shape from felt for center of coaster. Matching edges, cut shapes from assorted scraps of felt to cover web side of backing; fuse in place. Trace star pattern, page 143, onto tracing paper and cut out. Pin pattern to coaster and cut out star. Using 3 strands of embroidery floss, work *Blanket Stitches*, page 129, along edges of coaster.

NEEDLEPOINT "FRIENDS" PILLOW

Make one of your best friends feel extra-special with her very own friendship pillow, hand-stitched by you just for her! Choose your own color combination, or use the colors shown and follow the stitching chart on page 149 to stitch the design on 12 count canvas using needlepoint yarn. Sew heart-shaped buttons to stitched piece. Cut a piece of coordinating fabric and the stitched piece 1/2" larger on all sides than stitched area. Matching right sides and leaving an opening at bottom for stuffing, sew the pieces together along the stitched area edge. Turn the pillow right-side out, lightly stuff with polyester fiberfill and sew the opening closed.

65

MADE JUST FOR YOU

You'll be everyone's favorite "tailor" when you customize ready-made slippers, caps or even baby bibs with carefully chosen appliqué shapes! Don't forget the finishing touches…simple embroidery, buttons and rick-rack. See page 125 to decorate the slippers.

GINGERBREAD BOY BIB AND DOLL
BIB

- paper-backed fusible web
- brown felt and red fabric
- tissue paper
- pinking shears
- white and red baby rick-rack
- white embroidery floss
- baby bib
- red medium rick-rack

Refer to Embroidery Stitches, page 129, before beginning project.

1. Trace gingerbread boy and heart patterns, page 132, onto paper side of fusible web. Fuse gingerbread boy to brown felt and heart to red fabric. Use pinking shears to cut out appliqués; arrange and fuse on bib.

2. Sew pieces of white baby rick-rack across arms and legs. Using 3 strands of floss, *Whip Stitch* along edges of heart and gingerbread boy, work *Running Stitches* for mouth and eyebrows and *Satin Stitches* for eyes, nose and cheeks.

3. Sew red baby rick-rack on bib ¼" from edges; sew medium rick-rack to back of bib along edges.

(continued on page 125)

KIDS' HOLIDAY HATS

Purchased children's hats are really simple to embellish for stylish wintertime fun. Trace the desired pattern from page 149 onto tissue paper…use the pattern to cut shapes from felt scraps. Stitch the shapes to the hats with embroidery floss, then embellish with buttons. Top off the hats with a ribbon bow or a pom-pom made from several strips of felt tied together at the center. Make a different hat for each day of the week!

*C*hoose a gift wrap theme for each member of your family…angels, Santas, holiday plaid or gingerbread men are just right. Wrap each person's gift in "their" paper, and you eliminate the need for gift tags!

— Harriett Heppard
Drexel Hill, PA

*I*t's easy to dress up plain barrettes for the holidays with treasures from your button box. Just hot glue the buttons onto the barrettes, overlapping to completely cover. Great stocking stuffers for a little girl!

Christmas is Coming!

Reward little ones who've been on their best behavior with an early surprise. Our stuffed snowman is perfect for cuddling, and Santa keeps a watchful eye on the Christmas countdown board. See page 125 to make the snowman.

SANTA COUNTDOWN

This is a cute project to help anxious kids count the days 'til Christmas…just remember to let the paint dry between applications! Paint the frame of a small chalkboard green, then paint a red & white checkerboard along the frame…use a black permanent marker to outline the checkerboard. Trace the Santa patterns from page 154 onto tracing paper; use transfer paper to transfer the Santa to white craft foam. Paint the Santa…refer to *Painting Techniques* on page 130 for tips on *Shading Santa's beard*.

Use a white paint pen to write the words and draw "snowflakes" on the chalkboard and Santa. Use a craft knife to cut along the bottom of Santa's beard; arrange and glue Santa pieces at the top of the frame. Tie red & white ribbons together into a bow…leave one streamer really long. Glue the knot of the bow at the bottom of the frame, then tie a piece of chalk at the end of the long streamer. The kids will be ready to begin next year's Christmas countdown on December 26th!

PAMPERED PETS

Make sure your four-legged friends have a happy holiday, too! Braid Christmas-print fabrics into ropes for pulling and chewing, or hang an appliquéd stocking for Santa to fill with treats, toys and a new collar.

PET STOCKINGS

Follow *Making Patterns*, page 130, to trace the stocking pattern, page 152, and desired animal patterns, page 153, onto tracing paper. For each stocking, use the patterns to cut two stocking pieces from polar fleece and animal pieces from desired colors of felt. Arrange and pin the animal body on one stocking piece. Using a small zigzag stitch, sew body to stocking. Using floss to match felt colors, stitch remaining animal pieces on stocking. Referring to *Embroidery Stitches*, page 129, use 2 strands of black floss to work a *French Knot* for each eye, *Straight Stitches* for the cat's whiskers and *Running Stitches* for the cat's mouth. Add a bell, or two or three, to the collar.

Matching right sides, sew the stocking pieces together, then turn right-side out. For the cuff, cut a 7"x13" piece from a coordinating color of polar fleece; sew the short ends of the cuff together. Matching wrong sides and raw edges, fold the cuff in half. Matching raw edges, place the cuff inside the stocking and sew cuff to stocking. Turn the cuff to the right side, then sew buttons on the cuff. For the hanger, knot the ends of an 8-inch length of ribbon together...sew the knot inside the stocking at the heel-side of the stocking.

RAG CHEW TOYS

Your pets are family, too! Make their Christmas morning special by making them one of these rag chew toys. For the dog toy, tear three 12"x43" strips of fabric, braid tightly and tie a knot about 2" from each end...tear the tail ends into narrower strips. For the cat toy, tear three 3"x60" strips from fabrics. Thread the strips through a plastic ring and tightly braid the strips together. Knot the braid about 3" from the end. Tear the tail strips into narrower strips. Since these toys are so simple, why not make extras to donate to your local animal shelter?

After a wintertime walk, wash your pet's paws with a washcloth dipped in lukewarm water. Salt and chemicals used for melting ice on sidewalks and roads can irritate tender footpads.

Any dog lover will appreciate this gift! Fill a galvanized tub, perfect for bath time, with a bottle of pet shampoo, chew toys, treats, a grooming brush and coupons for dog sitting.

A Dog is the only thing on earth that loves you more than he loves himself. — JOSH BILLINGS

Yummy Gifts from the Kitchen

'Tis the time of year for making and sharing yummy treats! Holly's giving bottles of her special stir-fry sauce this year, and Mary Elizabeth has been busy putting together layered cookie mixes for her neighbors. Kate got an early start on making fudge to pack in decorated boxes, but then she ate it all and now has to start over!

Gift mixes are great for folks who love fresh-baked goodies but don't really have time to cook. It's so simple to prepare treats like Double Chip-Walnut Brownies when most of the ingredients have already been measured out! The brownie mix recipe is on page 85.

Recipe for: Double Chi
From the kitchen of:
Ingredients: 1/3 c. baking
2/3 c. sugar
1/2 c. chocol
1/2 c. vanill
2/3 c. brown
1 1/3 c. all pu
1 t. salt
1/2 c. ch

Tasty Treats to Share

There's no better time than Christmas to share tasty treats from your kitchen!

Decorate a jar with homespun, raffia and a star tag to hold a generous helping of Mollohan's Mix; see page 126 to trim the jar.

MOLLOHAN'S MIX

Looking for a gift for the kids' teachers? Snack mix packed inside a decorated jar will be a welcome gift.

1/2 c. dried apples
1/2 c. chopped walnuts
1/2 c. dried pears
1/2 c. colorful, candy-coated
   chocolate mini baking bits
1/2 c. dried bananas

In a one-pint wide-mouth canning jar, layer apples, walnuts, pears, mini baking bits and bananas in order listed. Makes 4 to 6 servings.

Pat Mollohan
Parkersburg, WV

CHRISTMAS CRANBERRY MUFFINS

Creates a wonderful aroma while baking, and so colorful, too!

2 c. all-purpose flour
1 c. sugar
1 1/2 t. baking powder
1/2 t. baking soda
1/2 t. salt
2 T. shortening
juice and zest of one orange
water
1 egg, beaten
1 c. raw cranberries, halved

In a large bowl, combine first 5 ingredients; blend in shortening. Add orange zest. Place juice from orange in a measuring cup and add enough water to bring liquid equal to 3/4 cup. Blend into flour mixture. Add egg and fold in cranberries. Pour into greased muffin cups, filling 2/3 full. Bake at 350 degrees for 15 to 18 minutes, remove from pan and cool on a rack. Makes approximately 18 muffins. This can also be made into quick bread by pouring batter into an oiled 9"x5" loaf pan and baking at 350 degrees for 50 to 60 minutes.

Beth Warner
Delaware, OH

CASHEW BRITTLE

Brittle is always a welcome gift.

1 c. butter or margarine
1 c. sugar
2 T. light corn syrup
2 c. cashew halves

Combine butter, sugar and corn syrup in medium saucepan. Bring to a boil over medium heat. Continue to boil 5 to 6 minutes or until candy thermometer registers 300 degrees. Stir in cashews. Pour quickly and spread on a baking sheet lined with greased parchment paper. Cool 15 to 20 minutes. Peel off paper and break into pieces. Mixture will be light in color and frothy before done (let it get darker). Makes about one pound.

Margaret Riley

Who could resist a batch of Cashew Brittle packed in a frosty snowman tin? Instructions for the painted tin are on page 126.

PARTY NUTS

Great to pack in a cork-topped glass canister and tie with a fancy wired ribbon.

³/₄ c. sugar, divided
1 T. cinnamon
¹/₂ t. ground ginger
¹/₂ t. nutmeg
¹/₁₆ t. ground red pepper flakes
¹/₄ c. butter
3 c. salted mixed nuts
1 t. water

Cover a jelly roll pan with wax paper; set aside. In a large mixing bowl, combine ¹/₄ cup sugar, cinnamon, ginger, nutmeg and red pepper flakes; set aside. In a medium skillet, melt butter; stir in nuts, remaining ¹/₂ cup of sugar and water. Cook and stir over medium heat until sugar melts and nuts start to brown, about 10 minutes. Stir nuts into spice mixture, tossing to coat; spread on prepared pan. Cool completely, then break into small pieces. Store in a tightly covered container at room temperature. Makes 3 cups.

Molly Bordonaro
San Antonio, TX

Oooey Gooey Yummy Popcorn Balls

EVERYBODY LOVES THESE STICKY TREATS! KIDS CAN HELP YOU MAKE THEM — IF YOU DARE!

1 c. light corn syrup
¹/₄ c. margarine
2 T. water

1 ¹/₃ c. powdered sugar
1 t. salt
24 large marshmallows
5 qt. popped corn, no salt

In a heavy saucepan, combine corn syrup, margarine, water, powdered sugar, salt & marshmallows. Stir until smooth and just comes to a boil. Remove from heat. Place popcorn in a large pan (like a roaster) and pour hot mixture over popcorn. Toss to coat. Let mixture cool a few minutes before handling. Wet hands with a very small amount of water and form popcorn balls. Press very firmly with hands when forming balls or they will fall apart! Place on wax paper to cool. Wrap in plastic wrap and tie closed with ribbon or yarn.

Fill a box with Heavenly Fudge, then photocopy our gift tag design on page 156 and hand-tint it using colored pencils...so easy!

Heavenly Fudge

12 oz. pkg. semi-sweet chocolate chips
6 oz. pkg. butterscotch chips
14 oz. can sweetened condensed milk
1¼ t. vanilla extract
1 c. chopped nuts

In a saucepan, combine chocolate & butterscotch chips with condensed milk. Melt over low heat, stirring constantly. When completely melted, add vanilla & nuts. Pour into a foil-lined square pan for easy removal & cutting. Chill. Cut into squares or with cookie cutters.

Oh, Baby!

CHEESE BONE COOKIES FOR DOGS

Don't forget your four-legged friends at Christmas!

2 c. all-purpose flour
1¼ c. shredded Cheddar cheese
2 cloves garlic, finely chopped
½ c. oil
4 to 5 T. water

Combine flour, cheese, garlic and oil in container of a food processor. Cover; whirl until mixture is consistency of coarse meal. With machine running, slowly add water until mixture forms a ball. Divide dough into 12 equal pieces. Roll out each piece to ½-inch thickness. Cut out using a dog bone cookie cutter. Transfer to ungreased baking sheet. Do not re-roll scraps. Bake at 400 degrees for 10 to 15 minutes or until bottom of cookies are golden. Carefully transfer bones to wire rack to cool completely. Refrigerate in airtight container. Makes twelve 4-inch cookie bones.

Nancie Gensler

HERB GARDEN BREAD

Enjoy this warm from the oven with real butter.

3 to 4 c. bread flour, divided
3 T. sugar
2 pkgs. active dry yeast
1½ t. salt
¼ t. dried marjoram, crushed
¼ t. dried thyme, crushed
½ c. water
¼ c. milk
¼ c. plus 1 T. butter, divided
1 egg

Combine 1½ cups flour, sugar, yeast, salt, marjoram and thyme in a large mixing bowl. In a small saucepan, mix water, milk and ¼ cup butter, heating until warm. Add to flour mixture and combine well. Add egg and enough of the remaining flour to make a soft dough. Knead 5 minutes on a lightly floured surface, adding more flour if needed to make dough smooth. Oil the inside of a large bowl and place dough inside, turning to coat. Cover and allow to rise until double in bulk. Punch down dough, and place on a lightly floured surface. Separate dough into 3 sections and allow to rest 10 minutes. Roll each of the 3 sections into a 30-inch rope; braid ropes together. Form into a circle, pinching ends together to seal, and place on an oiled baking sheet. Allow to rise until double in bulk. Bake at 375 degrees for 30 minutes, covering with foil if necessary to prevent overbrowning. Remove from oven, brush with remaining butter and allow to cool slightly before slicing.

For a quick and easy gift, cover the top of a jar of homemade preserves with brown paper and secure with a ribbon. Glue colorful buttons to the ribbon ends.

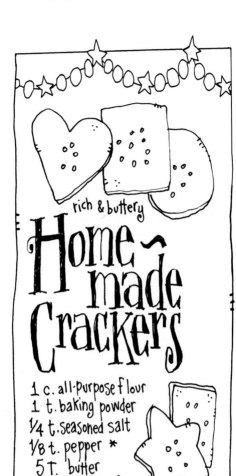

rich & buttery Home~made Crackers

1 c. all-purpose flour
1 t. baking powder
¼ t. seasoned salt
⅛ t. pepper *
5 T. butter
¼ c. half & half

Stir together flour, baking powder, seasoned salt & pepper. Using two knives or a pastry blender, cut in butter until mixture is crumbly. Stir in half & half all at once. On lightly floured surface, knead dough gently for about 10 to 12 strokes. Roll out ¼" thick. Cut with floured 2" round cookie cutter or other small shape ~ hearts are nice! Bake for 10 minutes on greased baking sheet at 400°. Split crackers open. With cut sides up, bake an additional 5 to 7 minutes 'til golden brown.

* You may substitute poultry seasoning, chili powder or garlic powder for pepper.

...wonderful favors for the office crowd!

 —where's mine?

HERBAL CHEESE SPREAD

Pack this spread in crocks...what a delicious gift!

2 8-oz. pkgs. cream cheese, softened
¼ c. whipping cream
1 T. olive oil
2 cloves garlic, minced
3 T. fresh parsley, minced
3 T. fresh chives, chopped
salt & white pepper to taste
⅛ t. dried thyme

Combine cream cheese and cream; beat until fluffy. Add the remaining ingredients and stir until thoroughly mixed. Spoon into crocks or other small, decorative containers and cover. This can be stored in the refrigerator for approximately 2 weeks.

Mary Murray
Gooseberry Patch

MICROWAVE PEACH BUTTER

So simple...you don't even need fresh peaches for this quick peach butter.

2 16-oz. cans peach halves, drained
3 T. powdered fruit pectin
¾ t. cinnamon
¼ t. allspice
2¼ c. sugar

Purée peaches in a blender or food processor. In a 2-quart microwave-safe bowl, combine peaches, pectin, cinnamon and allspice, mixing well. Microwave on high for 6 minutes, stirring every 2 minutes. Add sugar and mix well. Microwave on high for 5 to 6 minutes, stirring once. Microwave one more minute, then ladle into 4 clean 8-ounce jars. Cool slightly, cover and refrigerate.

Kathy Bolyea
Naples, FL

Surprise a snacker...pack a basket with a pot of Herbal Cheese Spread and paper-wrapped tubes of savory Homemade Crackers; the wrapper instructions are on page 126. Include festive cheese spreaders to add to the fun!

Holly's Oriental Stir-fry Sauce

1 T. GARLIC, finely minced
1 t. GROUND GINGER
2.⅔ c. WATER
¾ c. DARK CORN SYRUP
¾ c. SOY SAUCE
6 T. WINE VINEGAR
⅓ c. SESAME OIL
6 T. CORNSTARCH
2.¼ T. BEEF BOUILLON GRANULES
¾ t. ONION POWDER

Stir together garlic, ginger, water, corn syrup, soy sauce and sesame oil. Mix together well and set aside. In a large bowl, mix together cornstarch, bouillon and onion powder. Whisk in the vinegar until cornstarch is completely dissolved. Add soy sauce and oil mixture. Whisk until well blended. Makes 4½ cups. Sauce may be stored in refrigerator up to one month.

Fill a basket for the tea lover on your list with a bright red teapot, tea blends, a honey dipper and biscuits to snack on!

Holly likes to deliver her Oriental Stir-Fry Sauce along with a yummy recipe; you can photocopy our tag on page 156. Seal the bottle with wax (instructions on page 126) and use raffia to tie on a pair of chopsticks and the tag.

CRANBERRY-WALNUT APPLE BREAD

When you give this as a gift, suggest using half a loaf of the bread to substitute for half of the regular bread in a stuffing recipe…yummy!

2 c. apples, cored, peeled and
    finely chopped
3/4 c. sugar
2 T. oil
1 egg
1 1/2 c. all-purpose flour
1/2 t. baking powder
1/2 t. baking soda
1 t. cinnamon
1 c. cranberries, fresh or frozen
1/2 c. chopped walnuts

Grease and flour a 9"x5" loaf pan. Combine apples, sugar, and oil in a medium mixing bowl. Add egg, mixing well. Combine dry ingredients in a separate bowl. Add to apple mixture, mixing until dry ingredients are moist. Stir in cranberries and walnuts. Spread batter evenly into prepared loaf pan. Bake at 350 degrees for one hour or until a toothpick inserted comes out clean. Makes one loaf.

SAVORY BUTTERS

Try these wonderful butters on hot corn on the cob or fresh-baked homemade bread.

Parsley Butter
1/2 c. butter, softened
1 clove garlic, minced
1 t. fresh parsley, chopped
2 t. lemon zest, grated

Combine all ingredients in a small crock, blending until smooth. Keeps fresh in the refrigerator for 2 weeks.

Peppercorn Butter
1 c. butter, softened
3/4 t. pepper

Blend ingredients together, beating until fluffy.

Fines Herbes Butter
1/2 c. fresh parsley, chopped
1/4 c. fresh chives, chopped
3 fresh tarragon leaves, chopped
1/2 c. butter, softened

Mix herbs well. Add one teaspoon to butter, blending well. Add more herb blend, if desired.

Cocoa Oaties No Bake Treats

a recipe from Mel Wolk
* St. Peters, MO

1/2 c. margarine
2 c. sugar
1/2 c. milk
3 T. baking cocoa
1 t. vanilla extract
3.5 c. quick-cooking oats,
    *   uncooked

Bring margarine, sugar, milk and cocoa to a boil in a saucepan ~ boil for 3 minutes. Remove from heat; add vanilla and oats. Stir well and drop by half-tablespoons onto wax paper to cool. Makes about 4 dozen.

BALSAMIC MARINADE

Here's a gift for your favorite cook.

1/2 c. balsamic vinegar
2 T. scallions, chopped
1 T. fresh sage, chopped
1 T. fresh rosemary, chopped
1 c. olive oil

Combine vinegar, scallions, sage and rosemary in a food processor. Pulse and add oil until fully blended and smooth.

Pack up hand-labeled jars of Parsley, Peppercorn and Fines Herbes Butters in a ribbon-trimmed basket. *See instructions on page 127.*

Quick and Merry Mixes

These oh, so simple gift mixes are perfect for college students, busy moms or anyone!

CAKE IN A CUP MIX

Great for college students...a sweet treat anytime. Try different combinations to get your favorite flavors.

18¼-oz. chocolate cake mix
3.9-oz. pkg. instant chocolate
    pudding mix
3 c. powdered sugar, divided
4½ T. hot cocoa mix, divided
2¼ t. vanilla powder, divided

Place dry cake mix and pudding mix in a large mixing bowl; mix together. Divide and place ½ cup mix in 8 plastic sandwich bags; secure with twist ties and label as cake mix. Tuck one bag in a large mug that will hold at least 1½ cups of water. Because the cake is microwaved, be sure the cup doesn't have any metal decoration on it. Place ⅓ cup powdered sugar, 1½ teaspoons hot cocoa mix and ¼ teaspoon vanilla powder in 8 plastic sandwich bags; secure with twist ties and label as glaze mix. Place one bag of glaze mix with cake mix in each mug and attach the following directions to mix: Generously spray inside of coffee mug with non-stick vegetable spray. Empty contents of cake mix bag into mug and add one egg white, one tablespoon oil and one tablespoon water. Mix until well blended. Microwave on high for 2 minutes. While cake is baking, place glaze mix in a small mixing bowl and add 1½ teaspoons water; mix well. When cake is done, pour glaze over cake in the cup and enjoy while warm. Makes 8 to 9 cake mixes.

Cari Baker
Wayland, NY

During the holiday season, keep small bags of gift mixes on hand for drop-in friends. Cookie mixes are especially fun! Be sure to include the instructions with the mix.

A snowman mug is just the thing to hold a cheery flannel bag of Cake in a Cup Mix. To decorate the mug and make the bag and recipe card, turn to page 127.

ONION SOUP MIX

There are endless recipes that you can make with this popular mix!

³/4 c. dried, minced onion
¹/3 c. beef-flavor bouillon granules
4 t. onion powder
¹/4 t. celery seed, crushed
¹/2 t. sugar

Combine all ingredients and store in an airtight container; makes 20 tablespoons of mix. Add these recipe cards when giving as a gift:

To Make Roasted Potatoes: Toss 5 tablespoons soup mix with peeled and cubed potatoes and ¹/3 cup olive oil. Spoon onto a 15"X10" baking sheet and bake at 450 degrees for 35 to 40 minutes or until potatoes are tender.

To Make Onion Soup: Combine 4 cups water with 5 tablespoons soup mix; bring to a boil. Simmer, uncovered, for 10 minutes.

To Make Onion Dip: Blend 5 tablespoons mix with 2 cups sour cream. Stir well and refrigerate at least 2 hours. Stir again before serving with fresh vegetables or potato chips.

Iva Anderson
Tucson, AZ

Stitch up a cozy bag to hold your Onion Soup Mix; include the recipes for Onion Soup, Roasted Potatoes and Onion Dip. Instructions for the bag and recipe cards are on page 127.

JAMAICAN SPICE RUB

Great to make for a last-minute gift.

¹/4 c. cumin seed
2 T. coriander seed
2 T. chili powder
1 T. brown sugar, packed
2 T. kosher salt
1 t. cinnamon
1 t. cayenne pepper
2 T. black pepper

Toast cumin and coriander seeds in an ungreased skillet over low heat for 2 minutes. Place in a food processor and add remaining ingredients. Process until mixture becomes a powder. Can be stored at room temperature for 2 months.

Farmhouse Buttermilk Dressing Mix

1·½ T. dried parsley   1·½ t. dried tarragon
1 T. salt   1·½ t. garlic powder
1·½ t. dried chives   1·½ t. pepper
1·½ t. dried oregano   1·½ t. dried cilantro

Combine all ingredients well; store in airtight container. Give with these instructions! →

a tasty gift...

Pack a bucket full of fresh, fresh veggies: a bunch of bright orange carrots, stalks of crunchy celery and a crisp head of lettuce. Enclose a packet of home*made dressing mix!

FarmHouse Buttermilk Dressing

½ C. MAYONNAISE
½ C. BUTTERMILK
1 T. BUTTERMILK DRESSING MIX

Blend mayo and buttermilk; stir in dressing mix. Chill 'til ready to use.

SOFT DROP SUGAR COOKIE MIX

Friends will love receiving this easy-to-make drop sugar cookie mix!

4 c. all-purpose flour
1 t. baking powder
1/2 t. baking soda
1/2 t. salt
3/4 t. nutmeg
1 1/2 c. sugar

Sift together flour, baking powder, baking soda, salt and nutmeg until thoroughly blended; add sugar. Spoon mixture into a one-quart wide-mouth canning jar; pack firmly. Jar will be tightly filled. Secure lid and tie on the following instructions: Blend together one egg and one cup butter; add 1/2 cup sour cream and one teaspoon vanilla. Stir in dry ingredients from jar and chill dough overnight. Drop cookies by spoonfuls on an ungreased baking sheet. Bake at 375 degrees for 10 minutes or until lightly golden. Makes about 2 dozen.

Annette Ingram
Grand Rapids, MI

HARVEST SOUP MIX

Great to send in a care package to your kids away at college!

3/4 c. dried split peas
1/3 c. plus 2 T. beef bouillon
1/2 c. barley
3/4 c. dried lentils
1/2 c. dried, minced onion
3/4 c. long-grain wild rice
3/4 c. tiny bow tie or alphabet pasta

Blend together all ingredients and place in a one-quart wide-mouth canning jar; add lid. Tie on a gift card with the following instructions: Place soup mix in a large stockpot. Stir in 3 quarts of water, a 28-ounce can of diced tomatoes, undrained, and 1 1/2 pounds of stew beef, browned. Bring to a boil, then reduce heat and simmer, covered, for one to 2 hours or until peas, lentils and rice are tender. Makes approximately 16 one-cup servings.

Regina Wickline
Pebble Beach, CA

Wild & Crazy Rice Mix

Your Friends will GO WILD for this tasty rice blend!

3 c. WILD RICE
2 c. GOLDEN RAISINS
1 c. BROWN RICE
1 c. DRY LENTILS
1 c. BARLEY, QUICK-COOKING
3 T. DRIED PARSLEY FLAKES
1/4 t. PEPPER

3 T. INSTANT BEEF BOUILLON GRANULES
2 T. DRIED MINCED ONION
1 T. DRIED SWEET BASIL
2 t. DRIED MINCED GARLIC
1/2 t. GROUND ALLSPICE

— ★ —

RINSE WILD RICE, BROWN RICE & LENTILS IN COLD WATER. LAYER RICE & LENTILS IN LARGE BAKING PAN. DRY IN 300 DEGREE OVEN FOR ABOUT 15 MINUTES. STIR FOR EVEN DRYING. WHEN COMPLETELY DRY, REMOVE FROM OVEN and COOL. COMBINE COOLED RICE & LENTILS WITH REMAINING INGREDIENTS. STORE IN AIRTIGHT CONTAINER OR IN INDIVIDUAL 1-CUP PACKAGES. MAKES 10 CUPS OF RICE MIX.

INCLUDE THIS SIMPLE RECIPE WITH RICE MIX GIFT PACKS:

1 c. RICE MIX
3 c. WATER
1 c. SLICED MUSHROOMS

1 c. SLICED CARROTS
1/2 c. PECANS, TOASTED & CHOPPED

— ★ —

COMBINE RICE MIX & WATER IN A SAUCEPAN. BRING TO BOIL. COVER. REDUCE HEAT & SIMMER 30 MINUTES. ADD MUSHROOMS, CARROTS & PECANS; SIMMER 20 TO 30 MINUTES OR UNTIL TENDER. SERVES 6.

Deliver bags of Wild & Crazy Rice Mix tucked inside paper maché bags. Just glue on sprigs of greenery and pine cones for a festive touch. Hand-write the recipe on an index card, cut out with decorative-edge scissors and glue to a larger piece of red paper…so simple!

CHOCOLATEY-PEANUT BUTTER COOKIE MIX

Two of our favorite flavors in one terrific cookie!

1 c. brown sugar, packed
1½ c. powdered sugar
¾ c. baking cocoa
1½ c. all-purpose flour
1 t. baking powder
¼ t. salt

In a one-quart wide-mouth canning jar, layer the first 2 ingredients, packing down as tightly as possible. Add cocoa and pack down, then wipe the inside of the jar with a paper towel to remove any excess cocoa from the sides. Sift together the flour, baking powder and salt; add to jar, packing down tightly. Attach a gift tag that reads: Cream together ½ cup butter, 2 eggs and ½ cup peanut butter; stir in dry mix. Shape into balls and place on a lightly oiled baking sheet. Bake at 350 degrees for 15 to 20 minutes. Makes approximately 2½ to 3 dozen cookies.

Kendall Hale
Lynn, MA

TRIPLE CHIPPERS

Give cookie dough with baking instructions for a quick-to-fix treat.

1 c. butter, softened
1 c. sugar
1 c. brown sugar, packed
2 eggs
1 t. vanilla extract
2½ c. quick-cooking oats, uncooked
2 c. all-purpose flour
1 t. baking powder
1 t. baking soda
6-oz. pkg. peanut butter chips
6-oz. pkg. white chocolate chips
6-oz. pkg. chocolate chips
1½ c. chopped walnuts

Cream together butter and sugars. Add eggs and vanilla. Using a blender or food processor, process the oats until they turn to powder. In a separate bowl, mix the oats, flour, baking powder and baking soda. Add peanut butter chips, white chocolate chips, chocolate chips and walnuts; stir into egg mixture. Drop by tablespoonfuls, 2 inches apart, onto an ungreased baking sheet. Bake at 375 degrees for about 7 minutes.

Kim Duffy
Sheridan, IL

Fun Things to do with SANTA'S HAT

1. Fill it up with zip-locked bags of homebaked goodies and deliver it to a neighbor... ring the doorbell, drop the hat and run!

2. Hang a row of Santa Hats on your mantel, just like stockings... personalize each one with a monogram, or tie on a name tag with a bright ribbon and a jinglebell.

3. Use a fuzzy red Santa hat under every plate at Christmas dinner... perfect placemats! (Just for fun, tuck a personal letter from Santa into each hat, or a gift certificate!)

4. A christmas bouquet of holly and greens looks pretty in an upside-down Santa hat on a door or tacked on a gate.

5. Make a very personalized gift "basket" in a Santa hat:
* Fill 'er up with dog bones for a favorite pup.
* Balls of red & white yarn and knitting needles slip right inside a hat for Aunt Sue.
* Golf balls, tees and a glove are great hat-stuffers for a golf enthusiast!

This sweet treat can't be beat! Nestle the fixings for Sweet Apple Buckle Mix in a festive baking dish (be sure to include the recipe!) and wrap it all up with cellophane; tie with raffia and slip in a wooden spoon. The bag instructions are on page 126.

SWEET APPLE BUCKLE MIX

Makes enough for a crowd…great for a hostess gift!

2 c. all-purpose flour
1 c. brown sugar, packed
1 c. long-cooking oats
1/2 t. cinnamon
1/2 t. salt
1/4 t. nutmeg
1 c. butter
1 c. chopped walnuts
1/3 c. cinnamon chips
4 21-oz. cans apple pie filling

In a large bowl, combine first 6 ingredients; cut in butter with a pastry blender. Stir in walnuts and cinnamon chips. Divide into 2 plastic zipping bags; store in refrigerator until ready to give as gifts. Share one bag of mix and 2 cans of apple pie filling with these instructions: Spread both cans of apple pie filling in a lightly oiled 13"X9" baking pan. Sprinkle topping over apples and bake at 400 degrees for 20 minutes or until mixture bubbles. Serves 12.

Cheryl Bierley
Miamisburg, OH

Merry Mochaccino Mix

a recipe from
Karen Moran
Navasota, TX

1 c. sugar
2/3 c. cocoa
1 t. cinnamon
1/4 t. nutmeg
2 T. instant espresso coffee
1/2 c. dry milk

Combine all ingredients in a mixing bowl and blend well; pack into tins or bags. Mix makes 2 1/4 cups ~ enough for 10 to 12 servings.

Here is the direction label for the gift

merry Mochaccino

3 to 4 T. mochaccino mix
3/4 c. milk

Combine mochaccino mix with milk in a saucepan. Bring to a simmer, whisk, and heat 'til smooth & frothy.

The morning cup of Coffee has an exhilaration about it which the cheering influence of the afternoon or evening cup of tea cannot reproduce.

—OLIVER WENDALL HOLMES

Make a present of flavorful coffee beans packed in a tin for a coffee lover...quick and easy!

DOUBLE CHIP-WALNUT BROWNIE MIX

Turn these into chocolatey mint brownies by just adding mint chocolate chips instead of vanilla chips.

1/3 c. baking cocoa
2/3 c. sugar
1/2 c. chocolate chips
1/2 c. vanilla chips
2/3 c. brown sugar, packed
1 1/3 c. all-purpose flour
1 t. salt
1/2 c. chopped walnuts

Place cocoa in a one-quart wide-mouth canning jar. Use a paper towel to remove any cocoa from sides of jar. Layer sugar, chocolate chips, vanilla chips, brown sugar, flour, salt and walnuts, pressing down each layer as tightly as possible before adding the next. Attach the following directions to the jar: Combine jar ingredients with one teaspoon vanilla extract, 2/3 cup oil and 3 eggs. Pour into a greased 9"x9" baking pan. Bake at 350 degrees for 25 to 30 minutes. Makes 9 servings.

Shelly Pitsch
Billings, MT

UNBELIEVABLY DELICIOUS!
Incredible Cobbler Mix

a recipe from Samantha Starks
MADISON, WI

1 t. BAKING POWDER
1 c. SUGAR
1 t. VANILLA POWDER
1 c. ALL-PURPOSE FLOUR

—*—

MIX TOGETHER ALL INGREDIENTS UNTIL WELL BLENDED. STORE IN AIR-TIGHT CONTAINER. GIVE WITH THE FOLLOWING RECIPE:

Incredible Cobbler!

4 c. BERRIES   1 c. BUTTER, MELTED
1/4 c. ORANGE JUICE
1/4 c. SUGAR   1 EGG
1 t. CINNAMON   COBBLER MIX

BLEND TOGETHER BERRIES, ORANGE JUICE, SUGAR & CINNAMON; POUR INTO A 13"x 9" BAKING PAN. COMBINE BUTTER & EGG, ADD DRY COBBLER MIX AND STIR WELL. DROP COBBLER MIXTURE BY SPOONFULS OVER BERRIES IN BAKING PAN. BAKE AT 375 DEGREES FOR 30 TO 40 MINUTES OR UNTIL GOLDEN.

OH. MY·GOODNESS THIS IS TRULY INCREDIBLE Cobbler!

No one can resist this "berry" Incredible Cobbler Mix. For delivery, pack the mix in a vintage measuring cup adorned with a fabric bow. To make the recipe card, follow the instructions for "Making a Tag or Label" on page 130.

Festive Feasting

As you gather 'round the table for your festive feast, remember that the holidays are more than just an opportunity to sample delectable dishes...they're also special times to enjoy the company of family & friends. From casual potlucks to elegant open houses and hearty Christmas Eve dinners, we've got the perfect recipes to round out your party menu. All you have to do is send out the invitations!

Family & friends will eagerly line up to enjoy delicious dishes like Cranberry Pork Roast, Herbed Rice Pilaf, German Green Beans and Feather Rolls that are as light as air! Recipes are on pages 91, 96 and 98.

Holiday Get togethers

Holiday potlucks mean everyone gets to show off their favorite dish. This year, why not try something new? You'll wow the crowd with these recipes!

Potato, Ham & Cheese Bake

POTATO, HAM & CHEESE BAKE

After I had my first son, a friend shared this delicious casserole with our family...we've loved it ever since!

2 c. cooked ham, cubed
1/2 28-oz. pkg. frozen O'Brien
   hash browns
3 T. butter
3 T. all-purpose flour
1 1/2 c. milk
10-oz. pkg. frozen corn
1/2 t. Worcestershire sauce
1/2 t. dry mustard
1/4 t. salt
1/4 t. pepper
1 c. shredded Cheddar cheese
1/4 c. bread crumbs

Brown ham and hash browns in butter. Whisk together flour and milk; stir in corn, Worcestershire sauce, mustard, salt and pepper. Heat until sauce thickens. Spoon into an 8"x8" baking dish; top with cheese and bread crumbs. Bake, uncovered, at 375 degrees for 30 minutes. Serves 4 to 6.

Bobbi Carney
Aurora, CO

BAKED ZUCCHINI GRATIN

Double the recipe for a terrific potluck dish!

1 onion, sliced
2 lbs. zucchini, sliced
1/2 cup butter, melted and divided
2 c. shredded mozzarella cheese
1/2 c. bread crumbs
1/4 c. grated Parmesan cheese

In a lightly greased 2-quart baking dish, layer onion and zucchini. Drizzle with 1/4 cup butter; sprinkle with mozzarella cheese. In a separate bowl, combine remaining butter, bread crumbs and Parmesan cheese. Sprinkle crumb mixture evenly over the top. Bake, uncovered, at 350 degrees for 35 to 40 minutes or until zucchini is tender. Makes 8 servings.

Heather Anne Kehr
Littlestown, PA

OLD-FASHIONED PORK CHOP BAKE

An easy one-dish recipe that can be made ahead of time, refrigerated and put in the oven before taking it to your next potluck.

6 pork chops
salt and pepper to taste
1 onion, thinly sliced
3/4 c. rice, uncooked
1 green pepper, sliced into rings
28-oz. can peeled whole
    tomatoes, undrained
15-oz. can tomato sauce

Rinse pork chops and pat dry. Lightly salt and pepper both sides of each pork chop and place in a single layer in a baking pan which has been lightly coated with a non-stick vegetable spray. Place one onion slice and 2 tablespoons of rice on each pork chop. Add one green pepper ring on top of each rice-topped pork chop. In a mixing bowl, combine whole tomatoes and tomato sauce. Pour over the top of pork chops, covering all rice. Cover and bake at 350 degrees for 1 1/2 hours. Serves 4 to 6.

Sue Martin
Delaware, OH

SIMPLE SPOON BREAD

A perfect recipe for the beginning baker!

1 c. cornmeal
3 c. milk, divided
3 eggs, beaten
1 t. salt
3 T. butter, melted
1 T. baking powder

Bring cornmeal and 2 cups milk to a boil in a medium saucepan over medium heat; stir often. Remove from heat and add remaining milk, eggs and salt; mix well. Add butter and baking powder; mix well. Place in a greased 9"x5" loaf dish. Bake at 350 degrees for 45 minutes. Makes 4 to 6 servings.

Dana Cunningham
Lafayette, LA

Corny Casserole

Corny Casserole
a recipe from Cindy Watson ★ Gooseberry Patch

3 eggs
1/2 c. butter, melted
1/2 t. salt
7-oz. box corn muffin mix

8 oz. sour cream
16-oz. can creamed corn
16-oz. can whole kernel corn, drained

Beat eggs with butter. Add salt, corn muffin mix & sour cream; beat well. Add corn. Bake in 8"x8" pan at 350 degrees for 30 to 35 minutes. Serves 8.

Potluck Christmas Eve...everyone prepares their favorite dish and no one person has to do all the work!

Porcupine Meatballs

SOUR CREAM-CHICKEN CASSEROLE

After every potluck dinner, I always have an empty casserole dish to take home. It is so simple to make and so delicious to taste!

8-oz. pkg. stuffing mix, divided
1/2 cup butter, melted and divided
8 oz. sour cream
10³/₄-oz. can cream of chicken soup
10³/₄-oz. can cream of celery soup
4 to 6 boneless, skinless chicken
    breasts, cooked and cubed

Layer half of stuffing mix and half of butter in the bottom of a 2-quart casserole dish. In a medium bowl, mix sour cream and soups; spoon over stuffing. Top sour cream mixture with chicken. In a medium bowl, mix together remaining stuffing and butter; spread over chicken. Bake at 350 degrees for 45 minutes. Makes 6 to 8 servings.

Windy Houser
Deltona, FL

POTATO & SPINACH CASSEROLE

If you need a quick and delicious casserole for a family gathering or holiday potluck, this recipe is perfect!

6 to 8 potatoes, peeled,
    cooked and mashed
10-oz. pkg. frozen chopped
    spinach, thawed and drained
8 oz. sour cream
1/4 c. butter, softened
2 T. chives, chopped
2 t. salt
1/4 t. pepper
1 c. shredded Cheddar cheese

In a large bowl, combine all ingredients except cheese. Spoon into a greased 2-quart casserole dish. Bake, uncovered, at 400 degrees for 15 minutes. Top with cheese and bake 5 minutes longer.

Barbara Bargdill
Gooseberry Patch

Freeze fruit juice and mint sprigs in your ice cube trays...so refreshing in your Christmas punch bowl!

Porcupine Meatballs

a recipe from
Gwen Grybauskas * Sykesville, MD

1 lb. ground beef
1/4 t. salt
1/8 t. pepper
1 egg, slightly beaten
1/2 c. rice, uncooked
1 T. onion, finely chopped
3 T. oil
14.1/2 oz. can beef gravy

Mix first 6 ingredients together and shape into golf-ball size balls. Brown meatballs in oil, then place in a casserole dish; pour gravy over meatballs. Bake, covered, in a 350 degree oven for 45 to 60 minutes or 'til rice is tender.

spinach pasta SALAD

a recipe from Sandy Benham ★ Sanborn, NY

1 c. cauliflower flowerets, steamed
1 c. mushrooms, sliced
½ c. Italian dressing
8 oz. spinach noodles, cooked & drained
1 c. ham, cooked & sliced
½ c. grated Parmesan cheese

In a large bowl, combine cauliflower, mushrooms & dressing. Add noodles & ham; toss lightly. Spoon into bowls, sprinkle with cheese & serve. Serves 6 to 8.

Save time...prepare holiday foods that can be made ahead, and if friends and family volunteer to bring a dish, let them!

FEATHER ROLLS

Just like the name...light as a feather.

1 pkg. active dry yeast
¼ c. warm water
4 T. butter, softened
1 T. sugar
¾ t. salt
1 egg
¾ c. warm milk
2 c. all-purpose flour

Dissolve yeast in water; let stand 5 minutes. Blend together butter, sugar, salt, egg and milk; add to yeast mixture. Beat until smooth; add flour and beat until well blended. Cover and set in a warm place for one hour or until double in bulk. Punch down dough and divide into 12 portions; roll each into a ball. Place in greased muffin tins, cover and let rise for 30 minutes. Bake at 400 degrees for 15 to 20 minutes or until golden brown. Makes 12 servings.

JoAnn

Common sense (HUH?) Food Safety

☆ Don't let meats sit out too long at room temperature. Keep hot foods hot! Crockpots & warming plates are great inventions.

☆ Likewise, make sure cool foods stay that way by using a cooler, or by serving in a bowl of ice.

☆ Don't let dogs drink from the crockpot.

Spinach Pasta Salad

Chocolate Chip Cookie Dough Pie

CHOCOLATE CHIP COOKIE DOUGH PIE

There is nothing better than chocolate chip cookie dough!

18-oz. tube refrigerated
    chocolate chip cookie dough
2 8-oz. pkgs. cream cheese,
    softened
2 eggs
½ c. sugar
5 1.4-oz. bars chocolate covered
    toffee candy, divided

Press cookie dough into an ungreased 9" pie plate. In a large mixing bowl, combine cream cheese, eggs, sugar and 3 crumbled candy bars; pour over top. Bake, uncovered, at 325 degrees for 30 to 35 minutes. Cool completely. Sprinkle top with remaining 2 crumbled candy bars. Keep pie chilled until ready to serve. Makes 8 servings.

Kay Bissell
Taylor, AR

"We may live without poetry, music and art; we may live without conscience and live without heart; we may live without friends; we may live without books; but civilized man cannot live without cooks."

— Owen Meredith

Fabulous Fruit Salad

a recipe from Nancy Molldrem
Eau Claire, WI

8-oz. jar maraschino cherries
2 pts. frozen strawberries, thawed
6-oz. can frozen orange juice, thawed
12-oz. can lemon-lime soda
16-oz. can pineapple tidbits, reserving juice
2 bananas, sliced
6-oz. can frozen lemonade, thawed

Mix ingredients together; pour into a 13"x9" cake pan; freeze. Cut into squares and place on lettuce leaves; serve immediately. Serves 12 to 14

Jo Ann's Potluck Surprise!

1 lb. chocolate-filled sandwich cookies, crushed & divided
½ c. butter, melted
24 oz. whipped topping
2 c. mini-marshmallows
1·⅓ c. sm. mints

Reserve ¼ c. of cookies for garnish. Combine remaining cookies with butter; press into ungreased 13"x9" baking dish. Fold together whipped topping, marshmallows & mints — pour over crust. Garnish with reserved cookies. Chill covered for 1 to 2 days before serving. Serves 16.

MARBLED PUMPKIN CHEESECAKE

This looks so pretty on a holiday buffet table.

$^3/_4$ c. gingersnaps, crushed
$^3/_4$ c. graham crackers, crushed
1$^1/_4$ c. sugar, divided
$^1/_4$ c. butter, melted
2 8-oz. pkgs. cream cheese,
    softened
4 eggs
16-oz. can pumpkin
$^1/_2$ t. cinnamon
$^1/_4$ t. ginger
$^1/_4$ t. nutmeg

In a bowl, combine gingersnap and graham crumbs with $^1/_4$ cup sugar and butter. Press into the bottom of a 9" springform pan. Bake at 350 degrees for 8 to 10 minutes. In a mixing bowl, beat cream cheese until smooth. Gradually add one cup sugar; beat until light. Add eggs, one at a time, beating well after each. Transfer 1$^1/_2$ cups of cream cheese mixture to a separate bowl and blend in pumpkin and spices. Pour half of pumpkin mixture into prepared pie crust. Top with half of cream cheese mixture. Repeat layers using remaining pumpkin and cream cheese mixtures. Using a table knife, cut through layers with uplifting motion in 4 to 5 places to create marbled effect. Bake at 325 degrees for 45 minutes without opening oven door. Turn off oven and let cake stand in oven for one hour. Remove from oven and run knife around sides of pan to remove sides. Cool and store in refrigerator.

Kim Schwarz
Howard, OH

Calorie-free club soda adds sparkle to fruit juices without adding calories!

..:♡ A Potluck Blessing ♡:..

May God bless our meal and grant us a compassionate and understanding heart toward one another.

- Mount St. Mary Abbey blessing -

...P.S. and thank you, Lord, for our country friends.

Marbled Pumpkin Cheesecake

Gather your Friends

For a nice change of pace, try a progressive dinner! Bundle everyone up and travel from house-to-house for each course, enjoying the holiday sights along the way. At the last house, serve desserts and coffee while exchanging little Christmas gifts!

HOT CRAB CANAPÉS

One of Mom's favorites; every time I make it, I think of home.

1/2 lb. crabmeat, shredded
8-oz. pkg. shredded sharp
    Cheddar cheese
2 eggs, hard-boiled and finely
    chopped
1/4 c. mayonnaise
2 T. onion, grated
1 T. fresh parsley, minced
1/8 t. garlic powder
salt and pepper to taste
20 slices bread

Combine crabmeat, cheese, eggs, mayonnaise, onion, parsley, garlic powder, salt and pepper; set aside. Cut each slice of bread into 4 squares. Spread each square with crab mixture and place on an ungreased baking sheet. Bake at 350 degrees for 10 to 15 minutes or until lightly browned. Makes 6 dozen.

DeNeane Deskins
Marengo, OH

Macadamia Cheesy Puffs

Macadamia Cheesy Puffs

...Frankly, my dear, these are delicious.

1 c. buttermilk biscuit baking mix
1 c. unsalted macadamia nuts,
    finely chopped
1 c. Gruyère cheese, shredded
1/2 c. butter, softened
1 egg, beaten
1/2 t. ground white pepper

Combine all ingredients and stir until soft dough forms. Drop by the spoonful on a greased baking sheet. Bake at 375° for 12 to 15 minutes or until very lightly golden. Cool on pan several minutes, then finish cooling on a wire rack. Store in airtight container.

Holiday Appetizer Tree

2 - 8-oz. pkgs. cream cheese
1 envelope dry Italian dressing mix
½ c. fresh parsley, chopped
12-inch plastic foam cone
Heavy plastic wrap
10-oz. pkg. bite-sized square crackers
2 jars pimento-stuffed olives
1 can large ripe olives
Cherry tomatoes
Wooden toothpicks

★ ALSO GOOD ON A TREE: COOKED SHRIMP, CARROT CURLS, RADISH ROSES, RED & GREEN PEPPER CUT-OUTS....

In a mixing bowl, combine cream cheese & dry Italian dressing until well blended. Set aside. Cover plastic foam cone completely in several layers of plastic wrap. Spread a thick layer of cream cheese mixture over plastic-covered cone. Sprinkle on chopped fresh parsley. Decorate tree with alternating rows of crackers, olives & tomatoes. Use toothpicks to secure veggies to the tree.

Holiday Appetizer Tree

CREAMY SPINACH & CARROT SOUP

This soup is a great beginning to any meal!

3 T. butter
1 c. onion, chopped
2 T. all-purpose flour
1 c. half-and-half
10½-oz. can chicken broth
1 c. carrots, shredded
10-oz. pkg. frozen, chopped
    spinach, thawed
¼ t. salt
¼ t. pepper
⅛ t. nutmeg
Garnish: orange zest

In a 2-quart saucepan, melt butter; add onions. Cook over medium heat, stirring occasionally, until onions are tender. Stir in flour until smooth and bubbly. Mix in half-and-half and broth. Add remaining ingredients. Continue cooking over low heat, stirring occasionally, until heated through. Garnish with orange zest, if desired. Makes 4 servings.

Gail Prather
Bethel, MN

Creamy Spinach & Carrot Soup

CHEESE-OLIVE DIP

Serve with crackers or chips.

1 c. shredded Cheddar cheese
1 c. mayonnaise
1/2 c. onions, chopped
1/2 c. black olives, chopped

Mix thoroughly and bake at 400 degrees for 10 minutes. Serve with crackers or chips.

Carriage House Bed & Breakfast
Southaven, MI

LAYERED APRICOT SALAD

Layer this in a clear trifle dish for a really beautiful presentation.

20-oz. can crushed pineapple, juice reserved
15 1/4-oz. can apricots, chopped and juice reserved
6-oz. pkg. orange gelatin
2 c. boiling water
1/2 c. mini marshmallows
1/2 c. chopped pecans

Drain fruit and keep juices in separate bowls. Dissolve orange gelatin in boiling water. Measure one cup reserved pineapple juice and one cup apricot juice; add to gelatin mixture. Stir in pineapple and apricots. Pour into a 2-quart serving dish and cover with marshmallows and pecans. Chill until firm.

Topping:
1 c. pineapple juice
1 c. apricot juice
1 egg, beaten
1/2 c. sugar
2 T. all-purpose flour
2 T. shortening
1/2 pt. whipping cream, whipped

Combine juices, egg, sugar and flour. Cook over medium heat until mixture thickens; stir constantly. Add shortening, stir to blend and refrigerate until cool. Fold in whipped cream and spread over chilled gelatin. Makes 10 servings.

Kathy McEntyre
Stinnett, TX

Granny's Tater Soup

a recipe from Amy O'Connell
★ New Ulm, MN

6 potatoes, peeled & chopped
2 leeks, chopped
2 carrots, chopped
1 stalk celery, chopped
4 cubes chicken bouillon
1 T. parsley flakes
5 c. water
1 T. salt
1/3 c. butter
chives to taste, chopped
12-oz. can evaporated milk

Place all ingredients, except chives & milk, in a 4-quart slow cooker. Cover and cook on low for 7 to 8 hours or on high for 3 to 4 hours. Stir in milk and chives during the last hour of cooking. Makes 8 to 10 servings.

WOW!

HERBED RICE PILAF

I often add shredded chicken or turkey if I want a heartier side dish.

1/4 c. butter
2 c. long-cooking rice, uncooked
1 c. celery, chopped
1/2 c. onion, chopped
4 c. chicken broth
1 t. Worcestershire sauce
1 t. soy sauce
1 t. dried oregano
1 t. dried thyme

Melt butter in a saucepan; stir in uncooked rice, celery and onion. Sauté until rice is lightly browned and the celery and onion become tender. Transfer to a lightly oiled 2-quart casserole dish. Whisk together remaining ingredients and pour over rice mixture. Bake, covered, at 325 degrees for 50 minutes or until rice is tender. Makes 8 servings.

Jo Ann

GERMAN GREEN BEANS

My family loves this so much, there's never any left over!

2 14 1/2-oz. cans green beans, drained
15 1/4-oz. can corn, drained
1 t. seasoned salt
1 T. onion powder
1 clove garlic, minced
1 T. vinegar
4 to 5 T. olive oil
4 to 5 carrots, shredded
1/2 t. dried dill weed
1/2 t. dried oregano
1/4 t. dried tarragon
5 slices bacon, crisply cooked and crumbled

Mix all ingredients, except bacon, together in a large serving bowl. Refrigerate overnight, stirring occasionally. Top with bacon and serve at room temperature. Makes 12 to 14 servings.

Patricia Taylor
Wellsville, PA

mmmmm... the fragrance of orange peels!

ORANGE SALAD

Being a mom of four, I'm always looking for easy and refreshing recipes; this salad fits the bill!

5 c. red leaf lettuce, torn
1 red onion, thinly sliced
2 stalks celery, sliced
11-oz. can mandarin oranges, drained
1/4 c. slivered almonds
1/4 c. balsamic vinegar
1/3 c. peanut oil
1/2 c. sugar
1 T. Dijon mustard
1/8 t. salt

Toss lettuce, onion, celery, oranges and almonds together in a large serving bowl. In a mixing bowl, whisk together vinegar, oil, sugar, mustard and salt. Pour over lettuce mixture. Makes 6 to 8 servings.

Terrianne Grant
Sewickley, PA

SWEET ONION CASSEROLE

I make this dish year 'round.

5 sweet onions, sliced
1 stick butter
4 c. shredded Cheddar cheese
2 c. round, buttery crackers, crushed

In a medium skillet, sauté onions in butter until clear. Place 1/2 of onions in an ungreased 2-quart baking dish; spread 1/2 of cheese over onions. Sprinkle 1/2 of crackers over all; repeat. Bake, uncovered, at 350 degrees for 30 minutes. Makes 8 servings.

Karen Cary
Marshalltown, IA

Mommy's Hot Slaw circa 1967

STOP DREAMING and START EATING !!

Mom's HOT Slaw

1 medium head cabbage
2 carrots, shredded
6 slices bacon
2/3 c. onion, chopped
1/4 c. brown sugar, packed
1/4 t. dry mustard
1/4 c. cider vinegar
1/4 t. salt
1/8 t. pepper
1/2 c. salted peanuts, optional

Shred cabbage and toss with shredded carrots. Set aside. Dice bacon into small pieces and cook in large skillet 'til crisp. Remove bacon to paper towel to drain. Add chopped onion ∽ cook 'til tender. Mix in brown sugar, dry mustard, vinegar, salt & pepper. When sugar is dissolved & mixture is hot, add cabbage mixture & peanuts. Stir until well-combined but not cooked. Add bacon pieces ∽ serve immediately.

Orange Salad

"All cooks, like all great artists, must have an audience worth cooking for."

— André Simon

CRANBERRY PORK ROAST

Slices of tender pork roast make this a meal everyone will rush to the table for!

2¹/₂ to 3-lb. boneless pork loin
    roast
16-oz. can jellied cranberry sauce
¹/₂ c. sugar
¹/₂ c. cranberry juice
1 t. dry mustard
¹/₄ t. ground cloves
2 T. cornstarch
2 T. cold water
salt to taste

Place pork roast in a slow cooker. In a medium bowl, mash cranberry sauce; stir in sugar, cranberry juice, mustard and cloves. Pour over roast. Cover and cook on low for 6 to 8 hours or until meat is tender. Remove roast and keep warm. Skim fat from juices; discard. Add broth to a 2-cup measuring cup, adding water if necessary to equal 2 cups total liquid. Pour into saucepan and bring to a boil over medium-high heat. Combine cornstarch and cold water to make a paste; stir into saucepan. Cook and stir until thickened. Season with salt. Serve over sliced pork. Makes 4 to 6 servings.

Andrea Purdon
Redding, CA

CRANBERRY RELISH

Cranberry relish with a kick!

2 c. cranberries
1 onion, coarsely chopped
³/₄ c. sour cream
2 T. prepared horseradish
¹/₂ c. sugar

Chop berries and onion in food processor. Add remaining ingredients and mix. Place in an airtight container and freeze until ready to serve. One hour before serving, set in refrigerator to thaw.

Diane Stegall
Bedford, TX

Twisty Rolls

TWISTY ROLLS

I have been making these for years…but my dear Aunt Betty will always be the undisputed world champion Twisty Roll maker!

1 pkg. active yeast
¹/₄ c. warm water
3 T. sugar
2 t. salt
4¹/₄ c. all purpose flour, divided
¹/₄ c. butter, melted
³/₄ c. milk
1 egg, lightly beaten
1 T. water
1 egg, beaten
1 c. powdered sugar, sifted
2 T. milk

Dissolve yeast in water; set aside. Mix sugar, salt and 2 cups flour. Add dissolved yeast, melted butter and milk. Stir until smooth. Beat in egg. Add enough flour to make a soft dough. Knead in remaining flour until dough is smooth and elastic (about 5 minutes). Place in greased bowl and let rise in a warm place until double, about 40 minutes. Punch down and roll out to a ¹/₄-inch thickness. Cut into strips, about ¹/₂-inch by 6 inches and braid 3 strips together to form a roll. Combine 1 T. water and remaining egg. Place braids on a baking sheet and brush with egg mixture. Let rise an additional 15 to 20 minutes. Bake at 375 degrees for 10 to 12 minutes. Blend together powdered sugar and milk until a glaze consistency. When cool, frost. Makes 2 dozen.

Debi Gilpin
Bluefield, WV

*C*ranberries freeze nicely in a plastic bag. Use in recipes without thawing.

— Amy Schueddig
Imperial, MO

The most important things to do in this world are to get something to EAT, something to DRINK and Somebody to LOVE you.

— Brendan Behan

ORANGE-PECAN CORNISH HENS

Great to make during the busy holiday season. It's ready in less than an hour and is perfect served with wild rice.

½ c. butter, melted and divided
4 Cornish game hens
   (1½ lbs. each)
1 t. salt
1 t. pepper
½ c. orange marmalade
¼ c. orange juice
1 t. cornstarch
½ c. chopped pecans

Spread one tablespoon butter equally over hens; season with salt and pepper. Tie ends of legs together, if desired, and place on a ightly greased rack in a roasting pan. Bake at 400 degrees for 1 hour or until a meat thermometer inserted into meaty part of thigh registers 180 degrees. Blend together remaining butter, orange marmalade and orange juice; bring to a boil. Blend together a small amount of cornstarch and water, slowly adding remaining cornstarch until mixture thickens. Slowly add cornstarch mixture to marmalade, stirring constantly; add pecans. Place hens in a 15"x10" baking dish. Pour glaze over chicken and bake for an additional 10 minutes or until glaze begins to brown.

Erin Doell
Chicago, IL

Orange-Pecan Cornish Hens

Cover your buffet table with gift wrap...what a clever tablecloth, and so festive!

PA·RUM·PA·PA·PUM·

SCALLOPS & SHRIMP WITH LINGUINE

Everyone will love this!

1 lb. large shrimp
10 oz. linguine, cooked and hot
3 T. butter or margarine, divided
3 T. olive oil, divided
3 cloves garlic, minced and divided
1 lb. fresh sea scallops
8 oz. pkg. fresh mushrooms, sliced
2 c. fresh snow peas, trimmed
2 tomatoes, chopped
1/2 c. green onion, chopped
1 t. salt
1/2 t. crushed red pepper
1/4 c. fresh parsley, chopped
2 T. fresh basil, chopped
Parmesan cheese, grated

Peel shrimp; devein, if desired. Set aside. Heat 1 tablespoon each of butter and olive oil in a large skillet over medium-high heat. Add shrimp and half of garlic; cook 2 to 3 minutes or until shrimp turn pink. Remove shrimp from skillet; keep warm. Repeat procedure with scallops. Heat remaining 1 tablespoon each of butter and oil in same skillet over medium heat. Add mushrooms, snow peas, tomatoes, green onion, salt, pepper, parsley and basil; cook 4 to 5 minutes. In a large bowl, combine linguine, mushroom mixture, shrimp and scallops; toss well. Serve with Parmesan cheese.

Amy Biermann
Riverside, OH

BROCCOLI BAKE

A speedy side dish to make for a progressive dinner.

3 eggs
1 c. all-purpose flour
1 c. milk
1 onion, chopped
3 c. shredded Cheddar cheese
10-oz. pkg. frozen, chopped broccoli, thawed
1 t. baking powder

In a large mixing bowl, combine all ingredients. Place in a greased 13"x9" baking dish. Bake, uncovered, at 350 degrees for 35 minutes. Makes 2 to 4 servings.

Laura Strausberger
Roswell, GA

For easy-to-make decorations, dip small pine cones in copper paint. When dry, scatter them among the hors d'oeuvres on your buffet table.

Scallops & Shrimp with Linguine

HOLIDAY SWEET POTATOES

Save your scooped-out potatoes, mash and serve with leftovers!

20-oz. can whole sweet potatoes
16-oz. pkg. fresh cranberries
2 apples, peeled, cored and
    chopped
1/2 c. water, divided
1 c. sugar
1 c. chopped walnuts
1 c. brown sugar, packed
1 T. plus 1/2 c. butter, divided

Drain sweet potatoes and lay on wax paper. Scoop out centers of potatoes; set aside. Combine cranberries, apples and 1/4 cup of water together in a saucepan, adding sugar to taste. Cook over medium heat for 10 to 15 minutes or until cranberries burst. Add walnuts and stir well. Fill the center of each sweet potato with cranberry mixture and place in a baking dish. Combine brown sugar and one tablespoon butter in a small saucepan. Add remaining 1/2 cup water slowly to create a syrup. Cook over medium heat until thick. Drizzle over potatoes and dot with remaining 1/2 cup butter. Bake at 325 degrees for 15 to 20 minutes or just until heated through; don't overbake.

Cindy Watson
Gooseberry Patch

Butternut Squash Soup

Butternut Squash Soup

a recipe from Tina Stidam
Delaware, OH

2.1/2 lbs. butternut squash, halved, seeded, peeled & cubed
2 c. leeks, chopped
2 Granny Smith apples, peeled, cored & diced

2 14.1/2 oz. cans chicken broth
1 c. water
Seasoned salt & white pepper to taste
Garnish: freshly ground nutmeg and sour cream

Combine squash, leeks, apples, broth & water in a 4-quart slow cooker. Cover and cook on low for 6 to 7 hours or until squash and leeks are tender. Increase temperature to high heat. Carefully purée the hot soup, in 3 or 4 batches, in a food processor or blender until smooth. Return the puréed soup to the slow cooker. Season with salt and pepper. Cover and continue to cook on high heat an additional 30 minutes. Garnish with nutmeg and sour cream. Serves 8.

CHECKERBOARD CAKE

This fun cake, shown on our cover, uses a checkerboard cake pan set.

2 18¼-oz. white cake mixes
2⅓ c. water
6 egg whites
¼ c. oil
2 1-oz. jars red paste
   food coloring

Combine cake mixes, water, egg whites and oil in a large bowl. Mix according to package instructions. Transfer 4 cups of batter to another bowl; tint with 1½ jars of the food coloring. Transfer 3 cups of batter to another bowl and leave plain. Use the remaining batter to make cupcakes! Following package instructions for checkerboard cake pan set, spoon batters into greased cake pans. Bake at 350 degrees for 25 to 35 minutes. Cool 15 minutes in pans and remove from pans. Cool completely before frosting.

Frosting:
6 c. powdered sugar
1 c. vegetable shortening
7 to 9 T. milk
2 t. clear vanilla extract
¼ t. salt
Garnish: peppermint candies and
   fresh peppermint leaves

Make 2 recipes of frosting. Combine powdered sugar, shortening, milk, vanilla, and salt; beat until smooth. Alternating layers, spread one cup of frosting between each layer. Frost sides and top of cake. Garnish with candies and peppermint leaves.

MAPLE-SPICE PECAN PIE

The sweet maple flavor makes this pie special.

1 9-inch refrigerated pie crust
3 eggs
¾ c. brown sugar, packed
1 c. maple syrup
3 T. butter, melted
1 T. lemon juice
1 t. vanilla extract
¾ t. nutmeg
¼ t. salt
1½ c. chopped pecans

Place pie crust in a pie pan; set aside. In a large bowl, whisk eggs and brown sugar. Add maple syrup, butter, lemon juice, vanilla, nutmeg and salt; whisk to blend. Add nuts and pour into pie crust. Bake at 450 degrees for 10 minutes. Lower to 350 degrees and bake an additional 30 to 35 minutes. Makes 1 pie.

Sharon Shepherd
Terre Haute, IN

Maple-Spice Pecan Pie

Did you know…the word "dessert" comes from the French "desservir," which means "to clear away," as in clearing away the dinner dishes before the sweet end to a meal!

SNICKERDOODLES

My mom always made these when I was a child, and I still enjoy them today!

1 c. shortening
1½ c. sugar
2 eggs
2¾ c. all-purpose flour
2 t. cream of tartar
1 t. baking soda
½ t. salt
2 T. sugar
2 t. cinnamon

In a bowl, cream shortening and sugar; add eggs and beat. Sift together flour, cream of tartar, baking soda and salt; add to first mixture. Shape into one-inch balls; roll balls in mixture of sugar and cinnamon. Place 2 inches apart on a lightly oiled baking sheet and bake at 400 degrees for 10 to 12 minutes.

Terry Anderson
New Orleans, LA

German Chocolate Cake

GERMAN CHOCOLATE CAKE

No visit to my grandparents' farm would be complete without a fresh glass of milk and a big slice of my Grandma's German chocolate cake!

18¼-oz. white cake mix
5.9-oz. pkg. instant chocolate pudding mix
1 c. milk
1 c. water
3 egg whites

Combine all ingredients in a large bowl and beat at medium speed for 2 minutes. Pour into 2 greased and floured round cake pans. Bake at 350 degrees for 25 to 35 minutes. Cool 10 minutes in pans and remove. Cool completely before frosting.

Frosting:
1⅓ c. evaporated milk
1⅓ c. sugar
4 egg yolks, beaten
⅔ c. butter
1½ t. vanilla extract
1⅓ c. flaked coconut
1⅓ c. chopped pecans

Combine milk, sugar, egg yolks and butter in a heavy saucepan; bring to a boil and cook over medium heat 12 minutes, stirring constantly. Add vanilla, coconut and pecans; stir until frosting is cool and spreadable. Frost cake.

Sharon Pruess
South Ogden, UT

Visions of Sugarplums

It's so hard to resist those mouth-watering sweets…and why should we? Christmas only comes once a year!

Pecan Pie Bars, Mary's Christmas Cookies

"The great thing about candy is that it has no redeeming social characteristics. Its only purpose is to please…to taste so sweet and so good that we simply have to go back for more."

— Irena Chalmers

PECAN PIE BARS

Wonderful little pecan pie bars you can't stop eating! Great for a church social or holiday cookie exchange.

1¼ c. all-purpose flour
½ c. plus 3 T. brown sugar, packed and divided
½ c. margarine
2 eggs, beaten
2 T. margarine, melted
½ c. corn syrup
1 t. vanilla extract
½ c. chopped pecans

Combine flour with 3 tablespoons brown sugar; cut in ½ c. margarine until coarse crumbs form. Press into an 11"x7" baking pan. Bake at 375 degrees for 20 minutes. While crust is baking, combine eggs, remaining brown sugar, melted margarine, corn syrup and vanilla. Blend in pecans and pour mixture into crust. Bake for 15 to 20 minutes. Cool and cut into bars. Makes 18 to 24 bars.

Linda Loar
McConnelsville, OH

MARY'S CHRISTMAS COOKIES

These are easy, yummy and perfect for a Christmas cookie exchange!

1 c. butter, softened
1 c. brown sugar, packed
1 egg
1 t. vanilla extract
2 c. all-purpose flour
¼ t. salt
8 1.55-oz. chocolate bars
½ to 1 c. chopped nuts

Cream butter and brown sugar together. Add egg, vanilla, flour and salt. Spread into a 15"x10" jelly roll pan. Bake at 350 degrees for 15 to 20 minutes. Remove from oven and place chocolate bars on top while still hot. Let chocolate bars melt; spread over top. Sprinkle with chopped nuts and cut into small squares. Makes 4 dozen.

Susan Bowman
Moline, IL

MILE-HIGH LEMON MERINGUE PIE

This pie is "mile-high" on flavor.

8 oz. sour cream
3 eggs, separated
4³/₄-oz. pkg. lemon pudding mix
1¹/₄ c. milk
¹/₃ c. frozen lemonade
    concentrate, thawed
9-inch pie crust, baked
¹/₄ t. cream of tartar
¹/₂ t. vanilla extract
6 T. sugar

Blend sour cream and egg yolks; stir in lemon pudding, milk and lemonade. Pour into a double boiler and cook, stirring constantly. When mixture begins to thicken, remove from heat and pour into pie crust. Beat egg whites, cream of tartar and vanilla until soft peaks form. Continue to beat, adding sugar, one tablespoon at a time, until egg whites are stiff. Spread over pie filling, making sure meringue touches edges of crust. Bake at 350 degrees for 12 to 15 minutes or until golden.

Scott Harrington
Boston, MA

Sour Cream Pound Cake

When rolling out sugar cookies to cut, roll out on powdered sugar instead of flour. It works just as well and adds to the flavor just a bit more.

— Bonnie Morris

Sour Cream Pound Cake

a recipe from Dori Williams ★
Port Republic, VA

1 c. butter
2·¹/₂ c. sugar
6 eggs
3 c. cake flour
8 oz. sour cream
¹/₈ t. baking soda
2 t. rum flavoring
2 t. almond extract
2 t. vanilla extract

Cream butter & sugar; add eggs, flour, sour cream & baking soda. Add flavorings. Bake in greased & floured tube pan at 325 degrees for approximately one hour.

★Strawberries make a pretty garnish!

Oh, cakes & friends
we should choose with care
Not always the fanciest
cake that's there
Is the best to eat!
And the plainest friend
Is sometimes the finest
in the end!

~ Margaret Sangster

GRANDMA'S BUTTERMILK PIE

Old-fashioned and simple.

¹/₂ c. butter, softened
2 c. sugar
3 T. all-purpose flour
3 eggs, beaten
1 c. buttermilk
1 t. vanilla extract
¹/₈ t. nutmeg
9-inch pie crust, unbaked

Cream butter and sugar together; beat in flour and eggs. Blend buttermilk, vanilla and nutmeg; stir into flour mixture. Spoon into pie crust and bake at 350 degrees for 45 to 50 minutes or until center is firm and set. Cool well before serving.

Stephanie Mayer
Portsmouth, VA

Southern Pecan Pralines

French Bread Pudding

A soul-satisfying treat the whole family will love!

INGREDIENTS:

5 c. cinnamon, French or rich egg bread, crusts trimmed & cut into cubes
3 T. butter, melted
2½ c. milk
½ c. whipping cream
4 eggs
½ c. sugar
1½ t. vanilla extract

½ t. cinnamon, or to taste if using plain bread
½ t. nutmeg
1 t. orange zest, finely grated (optional)
⅛ t. salt
powdered sugar

Butter a deep casserole or baking dish and fill with bread cubes. Drizzle melted butter over bread cubes. Whisk together milk, cream, eggs, sugar, vanilla, cinnamon, nutmeg, orange zest & salt in a medium mixing bowl 'til well blended. Pour over bread. Place baking dish in a large pan and place in oven. Fill larger pan with hot water until it reaches 'halfway' up the sides of the baking dish. Bake at 350° for 45-50 minutes or until knife inserted in center comes out clean. Before serving, sprinkle with powdered sugar. Serve warm or chilled.

Mmmmm

Use a pastry tube to pipe icing names on cut-out cookies...angels, snowflakes or reindeer. They make tasty personalized place markers for your table!

SOUTHERN PECAN PRALINES

While touring plantations in Georgia and South Carolina, I found a wonderful book that shared Christmas traditions of the old South. These wonderful pralines are reminiscent of that simpler time.

1½ c. brown sugar, packed
1½ c. sugar
3 T. corn syrup
1 c. milk
1 t. vanilla extract
1½ c. chopped pecans

Combine sugars, corn syrup and milk in a heavy 3-quart saucepan. Cook over medium heat, stirring constantly, until the mixture comes to a boil. Turn the heat to low and continue stirring until a little of the mixture dropped into cold water forms a soft ball or mixture reaches 234 to 240 degrees on a candy thermometer. Remove from heat and let stand for 10 minutes. Stir in the vanilla and beat for 2 minutes, using a wooden spoon. Add pecans and stir until creamy. Drop by tablespoonfuls onto wax paper to make patties about 2½ inches in diameter. Let pralines stand until firm, then peel from the wax paper. Makes 2½ dozen.

Juanita Williams
Jacksonville, OR

RICH RUM CAKE

There can be no holiday without a delicious rum cake.

4 eggs, separated
½ c. brown sugar, packed and divided
1 c. all-purpose flour
1 t. baking powder
¼ t. salt
⅓ c. butter, melted
1 t. vanilla extract

Beat egg whites until stiff; beat in 4 tablespoons brown sugar. Beat yolks with remaining brown sugar and add to egg white mixture. Fold in flour, baking powder and salt; add butter and vanilla. Pour into a greased and floured Bundt® pan and bake at 375 degrees for 25 to 30 minutes. Remove from the oven. Invert cake onto serving plate; poke holes in the top with a long wooden skewer.

Rum Sauce:
1/4 c. butter
1 c. orange juice
1/2 c. powdered sugar
1/2 c. rum
Garnish: chopped nuts or
　　orange slices

Melt butter in a small saucepan. Add juice and powdered sugar; stir until sugar is dissolved. Add rum and heat through. Drizzle sauce over warm cake. Garnish with chopped nuts or fresh orange slices.

COFFEE-TOFFEE COOKIES

I always make these cookies during the Christmas holidays; they're a hit for the annual cookie exchange!

1 T. instant coffee granules
1 t. vanilla extract
1 c. butter, softened
1 1/4 c. sugar
1/2 t. baking powder
1 egg
2 1/2 c. all-purpose flour
3/4 c. toffee chips

Stir coffee and vanilla in a cup until combined. Beat butter, sugar and baking powder together in a large bowl with electric mixer until fluffy; blend in egg and coffee mixture. Gradually beat in flour. Divide dough in half; roll each half on a lightly floured surface into about a 9-inch log. Wrap each log in plastic wrap and refrigerate about 4 hours or until firm. Cut in 1/4-inch slices and place on a greased baking sheet about 2 inches apart. Place 1/2 teaspoon toffee chips on top of each cookie; press in lightly. Bake at 350 degrees for 10 to 12 minutes. Makes about 4 dozen.

Mary Steiner
West Bend, WI

Sour Cream Drops

...good to the last one!

1/4 c. shortening
3/4 c. sugar
1 egg
1/2 c. sour cream
1/2 t. vanilla extract

1 1/3 c. all-purpose flour
1/4 t. baking soda
1/4 t. baking powder
1/4 t. salt
1/4 t. nutmeg ~ optional
1/2 c. chopped pecans ~ optional

· · · · · ♥ · · · · ·

In a mixing bowl, cream shortening & sugar. Add egg, sour cream & vanilla. Combine dry ingredients and stir into creamed mixture along with nuts. Chill for one hour. Drop by tablespoonfuls, 2" apart, onto greased cookie sheet. Bake at 425° for 7 to 8 minutes 'til lightly browned. Remove to wire racks to cool. Ice with Burnt Sugar Frosting:

2 T. butter (no substitutes)　　1/4 t. vanilla extract
1 c. powdered sugar　　　　3 to 4 t. hot water

Melt butter in saucepan until golden brown. Stir in sugar & vanilla & enough water to make a spreading consistency. Frost cookies.

Coffee-Toffee Cookies

BLACK RASPBERRY PACKETS

You could substitute apple butter for the preserves if you'd like; just add a dash of cinnamon and you've got another great treat!

1 pkg. active dry yeast
¼ c. warm water
¼ c. butter
1 c. milk
½ c. ricotta cheese
6 T. sugar
½ t. salt
4 to 4½ c. all-purpose flour
½ c. black raspberry preserves
½ t. cornstarch
1 egg, beaten
½ c. sugar

Sprinkle yeast in warm water; stir to dissolve and let stand until mixture foams, 5 to 10 minutes. Combine butter and milk in a small saucepan and cook until butter melts; cool to lukewarm. Blend into yeast mixture and set aside for 2 minutes. Stir in ricotta cheese, sugar and salt. Add flour, ½ cup at a time, until a dough forms. Knead on a lightly floured surface for 10 minutes. Shape into a ball and place in an oiled bowl, turning to coat all sides. Let rise until double in bulk, about one hour. Punch down dough and roll out on a lightly floured surface into a 20-inch square, then cut dough into 4-inch squares. Thoroughly combine preserves and cornstarch; place a spoonful in the center of each square. Moisten pastry edges with water, fold dough over to make triangle and pinch to seal. Place packets on a greased baking sheet and let rise 30 minutes. Brush with egg and sprinkle with sugar. Bake at 425 degrees for 10 minutes. Makes 25 packets.

Robin Hill
Rochester, NY

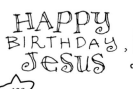

MARVELOUS MACADAMIA TARTS

You're sure to get "oohs" and "aahs" when you serve this!

½ c. margarine, softened
3-oz. pkg. cream cheese, softened
1 c. all-purpose flour
¼ t. salt
2 T. butter, melted
¾ c. brown sugar, packed
1 egg
1½ c. macadamia nuts, chopped
1 t. vanilla extract
⅓ c. chocolate chips, melted

Blend together margarine and cream cheese. Mix in flour and salt to form a soft dough. Chill at least one hour. Form dough into twenty-four 1" balls. Place each ball in a mini muffin cup. With flour-dusted fingers, press into tart shapes. Blend together remaining ingredients; fill each tart shell. Bake at 375 degrees for 20 to 25 minutes. Cool; remove from pan. Drizzle chocolate across tarts. Makes 2 dozen.

Nancy Ralston
Fresno, CA

Marvelous Macadamia Tarts

CREAMY PEACH PUDDING

Peaches and cinnamon just seem to go together.

5¼-oz. pkg. instant vanilla pudding mix
¾ c. all-purpose flour
¾ c. milk
15-oz. can sliced peaches, drained and juice reserved
8-oz. pkg. cream cheese, softened
¾ c. sugar
¾ c. powdered sugar
Garnish: cinnamon to taste

Blend pudding and flour; stir in milk and peach juice. Pour into an 8"x8" baking dish coated with non-stick vegetable spray. Place peach slices on top of pudding mixture. Blend cream cheese, sugar and powdered sugar together and spoon on top of peaches. Sprinkle with cinnamon and bake at 350 degrees for 30 to 40 minutes. Makes 6 to 8 servings.

Cathy Hughes
Cleveland, TN

CRANBERRY-APPLE PUDDING

This recipe is special to me because it always brings to mind the sweet aroma that filled Grandma's house as she was baking it.

4 apples, peeled, cored and thinly
   sliced
1 c. cranberries
¹/₄ c. raisins
juice and zest of one orange
¹/₂ t. apple pie spice
1 c. milk
1 c. bread crumbs

Combine all ingredients and place in a 2-quart glass baking dish. Bake, covered, at 350 degrees for 40 to 50 minutes or until firm in the center. Serve warm. Makes 4 to 5 servings.

Marie Brandt
Cold Brook, NY

CINNAMON PUDDING CAKE

A terrific dessert for a chilly winter evening. Serve with a mug of homemade hot cocoa!

1 c. sugar
2 T. butter
1 c. milk
2 c. all-purpose flour
2 t. baking powder
2 t. cinnamon
¹/₄ t. salt

Mix all ingredients together and blend well. Pour into a greased 13"x9" baking pan; add topping.

Topping:
2 c. brown sugar, packed
2 T. butter
1¹/₄ c. water

Combine all ingredients in a saucepan; bring to a boil. Pour mixture over the cake batter and bake at 350 degrees for 25 minutes. Serves 12.

Phyllis Peters
Three Rivers, MI

Stuffed Baked Apples

STUFFED BAKED APPLES
with Rich & Yummy Caramel Sauce

For one apple:

- 1 to 2 t. chopped walnuts or pecans
- 2 T. brown sugar
- 1 t. butter
- ¹/₈ t. cinnamon
- dash nutmeg
- 1 T. granola
- baking apple such as Rome Beauty, Winesap or Golden Delicious

Remove core & peel from upper half of apple. Place in oven-proof baking dish. Combine nuts, brown sugar, butter & spices; place in cored center of apple. Top with granola. Place about 1 T. water around apple in dish. Bake at 350° for 30-40 minutes. Serve warm with rich caramel sauce.

SAUCE:

- 3 t. cornstarch
- ¹/₂ c. cold water
- 3 T. honey
- 6 T. butter or margarine
- 6 T. brown sugar
- dash of cinnamon & nutmeg

Blend cornstarch & cold water in saucepan 'til smooth. Add the remaining ingredients to saucepan. Stir constantly ~ heat until it's thickened & boiling. Remove from heat and serve warm.

When baking holiday pies, use mini cookie cutters to make whimsical vents on your top piecrust...stars, trees or angels!

Mary Elizabeth's Butter★Pecan★Crisps

Mary Elizabeth's Butter-Pecan Crisps

2½ c. brown sugar, packed
1 c. butter, softened
1 t. vanilla extract
2 eggs
3 c. all-purpose flour
½ t. baking soda
1 c. chopped pecans, toasted
3 T. sugar

Beat brown sugar and butter in large bowl until blended. Stir in vanilla & eggs. Add flour, baking soda & pecans. Mix well. Shape into 1" balls. Place on ungreased baking sheet 2" apart. Flatten with bottom of a glass dipped in sugar. Bake at 375° for 8 to 10 minutes or 'til edges are golden. Cool on cookie sheet 1 minute, then move to wire racks.
Makes 72 cookies.

...A Hit with anyone within "whiffing" distance!

APPLE DUMPLING ROLLS

You can serve this wonderful apple treat warm or cold!

3½ c. tart apples, thinly sliced
4 T. plus ¾ c. sugar, divided
½ c. water
2 T. lemon juice
1 T. butter, melted
2 c. all-purpose flour
3 t. baking powder
¼ t. salt
¼ c. shortening
1 egg, beaten
½ c. milk
½ c. brown sugar, packed
¼ t. cinnamon

Combine apples, 2 tablespoons sugar and water. Boil for 5 minutes. Drain apples; reserve syrup. Measure ¾ cup syrup, adding water if necessary; pour syrup into 8"x8" baking pan. Stir in ¾ cup sugar, lemon juice and butter. Place baking pan in preheated oven while preparing rolls. In a large bowl, sift flour, 2 tablespoons sugar, baking powder and salt. Cut in shortening to resemble coarse meal. In a separate bowl, combine egg and milk. Add to flour mixture; stir with a fork. Transfer dough to floured board; pat into 18"x12" rectangle. Cover dough with drained apples. Sprinkle with brown sugar and cinnamon. Roll, jelly roll-style, and cut into 2-inch slices. Place slices, cut side down, in syrup in 8"x8" pan. Bake at 350 degrees for 35 to 40 minutes or until lightly browned. Serve with lemon sauce.

Lemon Sauce:
½ c. sugar
2 T. cornstarch
¼ t. salt
1 c. water, divided
zest of one lemon, grated
¼ c. lemon juice
2 T. butter

Mix first 3 ingredients in small saucepan. Add ¼ cup of water and blend. Add remaining water and bring to a boil; stirring constantly. Boil until thickened and clear. Remove from heat and add remaining ingredients.

Margaret Scoresby
Mount Vernon, OH

COCONUT CREAM PIE

So creamy and rich!

1 c. sugar, divided
6 T. all-purpose flour
1/8 t. salt
3 c. milk
4 eggs, separated
2 T. butter
1 1/2 t. vanilla extract
1 c. flaked coconut
9-inch pie crust, baked
Garnish: flaked coconut, toasted

In a large heavy saucepan, combine 1/2 cup sugar, flour, and salt. Over medium heat, gradually whisk in milk; whisk constantly until mixture is thickened and bubbly. Remove from heat. Beat egg yolks. Gradually stir about one-fourth of hot mixture into yolks; add to remaining hot mixture, stirring constantly. Cook, stirring constantly, over low heat 3 minutes. Remove from heat; stir in butter and vanilla. Stir in coconut. Beat egg whites and remaining 1/2 cup sugar until stiff peaks form. Pour filling into cooled pie crust. Spread meringue over hot filling. Bake at 325 degrees for 25 to 28 minutes or until golden. Cool before serving. Makes 6 servings.

Kimberly Davison
Nova Scotia, Canada

Apple Dumpling Rolls

Coconut Cream Pie

Beginning in early December, mix up batches of cookie dough to pop in the freezer. Jot down rolling thickness, baking directions, etc., on slips of paper and include them in the freezer bag. Saves searching for the right cookbook! When cookies are needed, all you do is bake them.

Soup's on!

On a cold winter's day, there's nothing more satisfying than a bowl of hot, hearty soup served with a generous portion of fresh-baked bread!

Black-eyed Pea Soup, Easy Cheese Bread

CARROT & POTATO SOUP

I have been making this soup for over 30 years. My mother made it for us when we were young, as her mother did for her.

6 c. water
1 onion, chopped
4 carrots, sliced
5 potatoes, diced
12-oz. can evaporated milk
1/4 c. butter
salt and pepper to taste

In a saucepan, combine water, onion and carrots; simmer until crisp-tender. Add potatoes; cook until tender. Blend in evaporated milk and butter. Continue to cook for one minute over medium heat. Salt and pepper to taste.

Pat Woods
Syracuse, NY

BLACK-EYED PEA SOUP

Add bacon, garlic and chilies to a classic soup recipe and you get this delicious variation!

6 slices bacon, crisply cooked and
    crumbled, drippings reserved
1 onion, finely chopped
1 clove garlic, minced
1 t. salt
1/2 t. pepper
4-oz. can chopped green chilies
4 15 1/2-oz. cans black-eyed
    peas, undrained

2 14 1/2-oz. cans beef broth
10-oz. can diced tomatoes and
    green chilies

Add onion, garlic, salt, pepper and chilies to bacon drippings; sauté until onion is golden. Add bacon and remaining ingredients. Increase heat to medium-high and bring to a boil; remove from heat. Makes 12 to 14 servings.

Kathy Grashoff
Ft. Wayne, IN

EASY CHEESE BREAD

A great accompaniment to your favorite soup or chowder.

2 1/2 c. biscuit baking mix
1 c. shredded cheese, any type
2 t. poppy seed
1 egg
1 c. milk

Combine first 3 ingredients. Combine egg and milk and gradually add to biscuit mixture. Stir vigorously until blended. Spoon into a greased loaf pan and bake at 350 degrees for 35 minutes.

Katy Bolyea
Naples, FL

Minestrone Soup

MINESTRONE SOUP

My aunt gave this recipe to me about 20 years ago. It's a wonderful main dish soup and it is very easy to prepare.

6 slices bacon
1 onion, chopped
1 c. celery, chopped
2 cloves garlic, minced
2 t. fresh basil, chopped
1/2 t. salt
3 1/2 cups water
2 10 3/4-oz. cans bean and
    bacon soup
2 14 1/2-oz. cans beef broth

2 14 1/2-oz. cans stewed
    tomatoes, chopped
    and undrained
2 c. zucchini, peeled and chopped
2 c. cabbage, chopped
1 c. macaroni, uncooked

In a large stockpot, brown bacon, onion, celery and garlic; drain drippings. Add basil, salt, water, soup, broth, tomatoes, zucchini, cabbage and macaroni. Boil until macaroni is tender. Makes 10 to 12 servings.

Linda Newkirk
Central Point, OR

BEEF, VEGETABLE & MACARONI SOUP

My mother and grandmother made this soup on cold, snowy days. Serve with homemade bread and jam!

1 lb. stew beef, cubed
1 t. oil
1 onion, diced
2 stalks celery, chopped
16-oz. can stewed tomatoes,
1 bay leaf
2 qts. water
4 carrots, peeled and sliced
14 1/2-oz. can green beans, drained
1 c. macaroni, uncooked

Brown stew beef in oil. Add onions and celery; cook until tender. Blend in stewed tomatoes, bay leaf, water and carrots. Simmer for at least 2 hours. Stir in green beans and uncooked macaroni. Bring to a boil and cook for 20 minutes. Add water if mixture begins to boil dry.

Pam Vienneau
Derby, CT

SPINACH-TORTELLINI SOUP

Tasty served with warm homemade bread.

2 cloves garlic, crushed
1 T. butter
2 13-oz. cans chicken broth
8-oz. pkg. tortellini, uncooked
1/8 t. cayenne pepper
1/4 t. black pepper
10-oz. pkg. frozen chopped
    spinach, thawed
16-oz. can stewed tomatoes,
    chopped and undrained
Garnish: grated Parmesan cheese

In a large saucepan, sauté garlic in butter over medium heat for 3 to 5 minutes. Add chicken broth and tortellini; heat to boiling. Reduce heat, add peppers and simmer for 10 minutes. Stir in spinach and tomatoes; continue to simmer an additional 5 minutes. Serve topped with Parmesan cheese to taste. Makes 6 to 8 servings.

Cindie Covault
Wilton Manors, FL

Cute Croutons!

A lovely little touch that only takes a minute or 2 extra!

Butter bread slices and cut into shapes using cookie cutters. Heat on a cookie sheet at 425° 'til toasty and crisp.

All's well that ends with a good meal.
—ARNOLD LOBEL—

FLOUR

WOODLAND ALTARS' WHOLE WHEAT BREAD

My husband and I met at Woodland Altars Camp over 16 years ago. We fell in love with each other...and this wonderful hearty bread! Excellent served with a spinach salad and white wine.

2 pkg. active dry yeast
1/4 c. warm water
2 c. warm water
1/4 c. honey
2 t. salt
3 T. oil
5 1/2 to 6 c. whole-wheat flour, divided
1 T. butter, melted

Dissolve yeast in 1/4 cup of warm water. In another bowl, combine 2 c. warm water, honey, salt and oil. Stir in 2 cups of whole-wheat flour, mixing well. Stir in yeast mixture. Add more flour, 1/2 cup at a time, to make a fairly stiff dough. Sprinkle a little flour on a board; knead dough 10 minutes. Shape dough into a ball, put in a greased bowl and grease top of dough. Let rise 45 minutes or until double in bulk. Punch down, divide in half and knead a little; let rest 10 minutes. Shape dough into 2 loaves and place in two 8"x4" greased loaf pans. Split top; drizzle with melted butter. Let rise until double in bulk, about 30 minutes. Bake at 350 degrees for 40 minutes. Yield: 2 loaves.

Carol Bull
Delaware, OH

Woodland Altars' Whole Wheat Bread

CORN CHOWDER

Spoon this yummy soup into individual bread bowls for a tasty change!

10-oz. pkg. frozen corn
1/2 c. potato, peeled and cubed
1/2 c. onion, chopped
1/3 c. water
1 t. instant chicken bouillon granules
1/8 t. white pepper
1 3/4 c. milk, divided
2 T. powdered milk
2 T. all-purpose flour
Garnish: 1 T. bacon, crisply cooked and crumbled

In a large saucepan, combine corn, potato, onion, water, bouillon granules and pepper. Bring to a boil and reduce heat. Cover and simmer about 10 minutes or until potatoes are tender, stirring occasionally. Stir in 1 1/2 cups milk. In a small bowl, stir together powdered milk and flour. Gradually stir in the remaining 1/4 cup milk until smooth. Stir the flour mixture into the corn mixture. Stirring constantly, cook until mixture is thick and bubbly. Cook and stir for one minute longer. Garnish with bacon pieces before serving. Makes 4 servings.

Kathy Grashoff
Ft. Wayne, IN

Great Garnish!

TOP A SOUP with:

Lemon or Lime Slices
Bell Pepper Rings
Popcorn   Cheese
      Animal Crackers
Toasted Nuts
      Bacon Crumbles
A dollop of Yogurt
   Alfalfa Sprouts
Corn chips   paprika
Hard-cook eggs, chopped
   Thinly-sliced carrots
Dill or parsley snips
      Sour cream
   whipped cream
      Crumbled crackers
      Tiny slivers of apple

HECK, SKIP THE SOUP & JUST EAT THE GARNISHES.

PARMESAN-ONION SOUP

A rich and flavorful soup that will warm you to your toes!

3 T. butter, melted
4 c. onions, thinly sliced
½ t. sugar
1 T. all-purpose flour
4 c. water
salt and pepper to taste
4 French bread slices, toasted
½ c. freshly grated Parmesan
    cheese

In a large saucepan, combine butter and onions; sauté until onions are tender. Stir in sugar and flour; continue to cook for 3 to 5 minutes. Add water and simmer, partially covered, for 30 minutes. Add salt and pepper, blending well. Fill 4 oven-proof bowls with soup; top each with a bread slice and sprinkle generously with Parmesan cheese. Bake in a 400 degree oven until cheese melts. Serves 4.

Zoe Bennett
Columbia, SC

CHEESY VEGETABLE SOUP

I think this is the best soup I've ever tasted…it's delicious!

4 10½-oz. cans chicken broth
2½ c. potatoes, peeled and cubed
1 c. celery, chopped
1 c. onion, chopped
2½ c. broccoli, chopped
2½ c. cauliflower, chopped
2 10¾-oz. cans cream of
    chicken soup
1 lb. pasteurized process cheese
    spread, cubed
1 lb. pasteurized process Mexican
    cheese spread, cubed
1 lb. cooked chicken or ham, cubed

In large soup pot, combine chicken broth, potatoes, celery and onion. Cook for about 20 minutes or until vegetables are tender. Add broccoli and cauliflower. Cook an additional 10 minutes. Add soup, cheeses and chicken or ham; simmer until warm. Makes 14½ cups.

Belinda Gibson
Amarillo, TX

Cheesy Vegetable Soup, Sour Cream Cornbread

"Beautiful soup, so rich and green, waiting in a hot tureen! Who for such dainties would not stoop? Soup of the evening, beautiful soup!"

— Lewis Carroll

BUTTERHORN ROLLS

These are the greatest!

1 pkg. active dry yeast
1 T. plus ½ c. sugar, divided
¼ c. plus 1 c. warm water, divided
1 c. butter, melted and divided
1 t. salt
3 eggs, beaten
5 c. all-purpose flour

Dissolve yeast and one tablespoon of sugar in ¼ cup water. Add one cup lukewarm water and ½ cup butter to yeast mixture. Combine with ½ cup of sugar, salt and eggs. Add flour, one cup at a time, mixing well. Cover and refrigerate overnight. Three hours before planning to serve, remove dough from refrigerator and roll into a ⅛-inch thick circle. Spread top with ¼ cup melted butter. Cut in wedges like a pie. Roll each piece, starting at larger end. Place on greased baking sheet, cover with a cloth and let rise in warm place. Remove cloth; brush with remaining melted butter. Bake at 375 degrees for 12 to 15 minutes.

Francie Stutzman
Dalton, OH

SOUR CREAM CORNBREAD

Easy to make!

1 c. self-rising cornmeal
8-oz. carton sour cream
3 eggs, lightly beaten
¼ c. oil

Heat a lightly greased 8-inch cast-iron skillet or deep-dish pie pan in a 400 degree oven for 5 minutes. Combine cornmeal and remaining ingredients, stirring just until moistened. Remove prepared skillet from oven and spoon batter into skillet. Bake at 400 degrees for 30 minutes or until golden. Serves 4 to 6.

Cathy Hurley
Poca, WV

Make-ahead Meals and more

We know you're just as busy as we are during the holidays...and just as short on time. That's why we've provided this collection of tried-and-true appetizers, entrées and munchies. They're easy to make, and they travel well, too!

Time-saver! Prepare your casserole the night before, cover and refrigerate. Be sure to add 15 to 20 minutes to the cooking time.

SLOW COOKER TURKEY & DRESSING

I like to start this before I leave for work...slice and serve when I get home!

8-oz. pkg. stuffing mix
1/2 c. hot water
2 T. butter, softened
1 onion, chopped
1/2 c. celery, chopped
1/4 c. sweetened, dried cranberries
3-lb. boneless turkey breast, cut in half
1/4 t. dried basil
1/2 t. salt
1/2 t. pepper

Coat a 4 1/2-quart slow cooker with non-stick vegetable spray; spoon in dry stuffing mix. Add water, butter, onion, celery and cranberries; mix well. Sprinkle turkey breast pieces with basil, salt and pepper and place over stuffing mixture. Cook on high, covered, for one hour; reduce to low for 6 hours. Remove turkey, slice and set aside. Gently stir the stuffing and allow to sit for 5 minutes. Transfer stuffing to a platter and top with sliced turkey. Makes 4 to 6 servings.

Geneva Rogers
Gillette, WY

BEEF & BARLEY VEGETABLE SOUP

This homestyle soup is one of my favorites because it's healthy and it freezes well.

1 1/2 lbs. stew meat
2 T. oil
1 qt. beef broth
1 t. salt
1/4 t. pepper
2 T. parsley, chopped
1/4 c. pearl barley, uncooked
1 c. carrots, chopped
1/4 c. onion, chopped
1/2 c. celery, chopped
2 c. tomatoes, cooked
1 c. frozen green peas, thawed

Lightly brown meat in oil. Place meat, broth, seasonings, parsley and barley in Dutch oven. Cover tightly and simmer slowly for one hour. Add carrots, onion, celery and tomatoes. Simmer for 45 minutes. Add peas and continue to cook for an additional 15 minutes.

Linda Charles
Delafield, WI

Beef & Barley Vegetable Soup

Chicken Tetrazzini

CHICKEN TETRAZZINI

This recipe came from one of my mother's best friends, "Aunt" Cathryn. She always served it for holiday dinners and now my mother makes it for us. I have wonderful memories of "Aunt" Cathryn; this dish brings her back for awhile.

1 onion, minced
2 T. butter
2 10³/₄-oz. cans cream of
    mushroom soup
2 10³/₄-oz. cans cream of
    chicken soup
8-oz. pkg. Old English cheese
1/2 c. milk
1/2 c. water
1 t. curry powder
1/4 t. dried thyme
1/8 t. dried basil
1/4 t. dried oregano
2 7-oz. pkgs. spaghetti, cooked
5-lb. chicken, cooked and cubed
4-oz. jar pimentos
salt and pepper to taste
1/2 c. grated Parmesan cheese

Sauté onion in butter in a Dutch oven. Add soups, cheese, milk, water and spices. Add spaghetti to soup mixture; fold in chicken and pimentos. Add salt and pepper. Spoon casserole into a 13"x9" casserole dish. Top with Parmesan cheese. Bake at 350 degrees for 45 minutes.

Debbie Musick
Yukon, OK

BROILED CHEESE ROUNDS

Make ahead and freeze...just spread bread with bacon mixture; freeze on baking sheets. When frozen, place rounds in plastic zipping bags; thaw for one hour before baking.

1 lb. bacon, crisply cooked and
    crumbled
4 c. shredded sharp Cheddar
    cheese
1 onion, minced
1 to 2 T. mayonnaise
2 loaves sliced party rye bread

In a medium mixing bowl, combine bacon, cheese and onion; blend in mayonnaise. Spread mixture onto bread slices; place on an ungreased baking sheet. Broil 3 to 4 inches from heat source for 3 minutes. Makes 2¹/₂ dozen.

Tammy McCartney
Oxford, OH

Be creative with leftover biscuits...spoon berries and whipped cream on them for a fresh dessert, or place a sausage patty and a cooked egg on one for breakfast.

APPLE-OATMEAL COFFEE CAKE

A tasty coffee cake any time of year, but especially good with just-picked apples.

1 c. all-purpose flour
³/₄ t. baking soda
1/2 t. salt
1/4 t. allspice
1/4 t. cinnamon
1 c. sugar
1 c. quick-cooking oats, uncooked
1/2 c. oil
1 egg
1 t. vanilla extract
1 c. apple, peeled and chopped
1/3 c. nuts, chopped

Mix dry ingredients together in bowl. Add remaining ingredients; mixture will be quite thick. Pour into a greased 8"x8" baking pan. Bake at 350 degrees for 35 minutes. Makes 9 servings.

Winnette Anker
South Holland, IL

Smell is a potent wizard that transports us across all the years we have lived. -Helen Keller

Great Grandma's Christmas Cookies

EASY REFRIGERATOR ROLLS
Delicious rolls that taste like Grandma's.

2 c. warm water
2 pkgs. active dry yeast
$^1/_2$ c. sugar
$^1/_4$ c. oil
1 t. salt
1 egg, beaten
7 c. all-purpose flour

Blend together warm water, yeast, sugar, oil and salt; stir in egg and flour. Mix well and place in a greased bowl, turning once to coat. Loosely cover with a cloth and let rise in a warm place until double in bulk. Punch down dough, cover and refrigerate until ready to use; dough will stay fresh for one to 2 weeks. When making rolls, shape into one-inch balls, placing 3 balls in each section of a buttered muffin tin; let rise until double in bulk. Bake at 400 degrees for 15 to 20 minutes or until golden. Makes approximately 3 dozen.

Zoe Bennett
Columbia, SC

GREAT GRANDMA'S CHRISTMAS COOKIES
This recipe has been in my family for over 100 years. My 2 sisters and I would stand on chairs pushed up to the counter on both sides of Great-Grandma Sunny. She would cut the cookies out with a round biscuit cutter and our job was to cut out a little circle from the center of each cookie with a silver thimble. After baking and frosting, the cookies were packed into tins and placed in the freezer until the week of Christmas.

2 c. brown sugar, packed
1 c. shortening
1 egg, beaten
$^1/_2$ c. buttermilk
3 c. all-purpose flour
4 T. baking cocoa
1 t. cinnamon
$^1/_8$ t. salt
1 t. baking soda

Cream brown sugar with shortening. Mix in egg and buttermilk. In separate bowl, combine flour, cocoa, cinnamon, salt and baking soda. Add enough flour mixture to the brown sugar mixture to make a stiff dough. Roll out and cut with a $2^1/2$" biscuit cutter. Cut a thimble-size center hole in the middle of each cookie. Bake at 350 degrees for 12 to 14 minutes. When cool, frost with your favorite powdered sugar frosting. Makes 3 dozen.

Stacey Weichert
Moorhead, MN

Morning Glory Muffins

MORNING GLORY MUFFINS
I like these because they freeze well. Just make several batches, freeze and then easily reheat whenever you want to enjoy.

2 c. all-purpose flour
$1^1/_4$ c. sugar
2 t. baking soda
2 t. cinnamon
$^1/_2$ t. salt
2 c. carrots, grated
$^1/_2$ c. flaked coconut
$^1/_2$ c. raisins
1 apple, peeled, cored and diced
$^1/_2$ c. walnuts, chopped
3 eggs
1 c. oil
2 t. vanilla extract

In a large bowl, combine flour, sugar, baking soda, cinnamon and salt. Stir in carrots, coconut, raisins, apple and nuts. In a separate bowl, beat together eggs, oil and vanilla. Stir egg mixture into flour mixture. Spoon into greased muffin cups, filling $^3/_4$ full. Bake at 400 degrees for 20 to 22 minutes. Makes 16 large muffins.

Cindy McAllister
Sheridan, MI

CHOCOLATE JAR CAKES

Tie with gift tags and pretty ribbons.

8 pint-sized wide-mouth
   canning jars
1/2 c. plus 3 T. unsalted butter
3 c. sugar, divided
4 eggs
1 T. vanilla extract
2 c. unsweetened applesauce
3 c. all-purpose flour
3/4 c. baking cocoa
1 t. baking soda
1/2 t. baking powder
1/8 t. salt

Wash canning jars (be sure to use the kind that have no shoulders) in hot, soapy water. Rinse well, dry and let them come to room temperature. Grease insides of jars well. Beat together butter and 1 1/2 cups sugar until fluffy. Add eggs and remaining 1 1/2 cups sugar, vanilla and applesauce. Sift dry ingredients together and add to the applesauce mixture a little at a time; beat well after each addition. Pour one cup of batter into each jar and carefully remove any batter from the rims. Place jars in preheated 325 degree oven and bake for 40 minutes. While cakes are baking, bring a saucepan of water to a boil and carefully add jar lids. Remove pan from heat and keep lids hot until ready to use. When the cakes have finished baking, remove jars from oven. Place lids on jars, and screw rings on tightly. Jars will seal as they cool. Cakes will slide right out when ready to serve. Store in the refrigerator and eat within 2 weeks.

Mary Murray
Gooseberry Patch

Chocolate Jar Cakes

... DID SOMEBODY SAY CAKE?

The YUMMIES ~ oh, the best part!

Sassy STRAWBERRY BREAD

1 c. butter
1 1/2 c. sugar
1 t. vanilla extract
1/4 t. lemon extract
4 eggs
3 c. all-purpose flour
1 t. salt
1/2 t. baking soda
1/4 t. cream of tartar

1 c. strawberry preserves
1/2 c. sour cream
1/2 c. chopped pecans

Cream butter, sugar & extracts together in big bowl. Add eggs, one at a time, beating after each addition. Sift dry items together. Add dry ingredients alternately with preserves & sour cream. Fold in pecans. Pour into 2 greased & floured loaf pans. Bake at 350° for 50 to 60 minutes. Let cool in pans 10 minutes before removing.

Here's a simple, easy dessert: buy a white angel food cake...slice and drizzle with ready-made raspberry sauce; top with whipped cream.

INSTRUCTIONS

MEMORY PAGES

(shown on pages 8 and 9)

With so many memories to preserve for tomorrow's generations, the ideas for personalizing recipe pages for each great (or not so great) cook in your family are limitless. Glue a piece of vintage fabric or decorative scrapbook paper to a piece of heavy card stock to fit in your album…punch holes down one side to fit binder. Use acid-free adhesive to attach photos, handwritten recipes, tidbits of advice or other mementos to the page…glue a snippet here and there from the honoree's apron, favorite tablecloth, dishcloth, curtains or hankie for a truly personalized memory page. Use a marker to add details to the page as desired.

FAMILY COOKBOOK ALBUM

(shown on pages 8 and 9)

- photo album with hardware attached to spine
- high-loft polyester batting
- vintage tablecloth
- hot glue gun
- dishcloth
- lightweight cardboard
- spray adhesive
- card stock
- fabric glue
- black ultra-fine-point marker
- colored pencils
- embroidery floss
- assorted buttons

Use hot glue for all gluing unless otherwise indicated. Allow fabric glue to dry after each application.

1. Measure height and width of open album; cut a piece from batting the determined measurement. Draw around open album on wrong side of tablecloth; cut out 2" outside the drawn lines.

2. Glue batting to outside of album. Center open album, batting side down, on wrong side of tablecloth piece. Fold, then glue corners of tablecloth diagonally over corners of album. Clipping top and bottom edges to fit under binding hardware, fold edges of tablecloth to inside of album and glue in place.

3. To cover inside of album, cut two 2" wide strips from dishcloth the same length as height of album; press ends ¼" to wrong side. With one long edge tucked under hardware, center and glue strips along each side of binding hardware.

4. Measure height and width of front of album; cut 2 pieces from cardboard ½" smaller on all sides than determined measurements; cut 2 pieces from dishcloth one-inch larger on all sides than cardboard pieces. To cover each piece, apply spray adhesive to one side of cardboard piece; center and place piece, adhesive side down, on wrong side of dishcloth piece. Fold and glue corners of dishcloth diagonally over corners of album; glue edges of dishcloth over edges of cardboard. Glue covered cardboard pieces inside front and back of album.

5. Cut desired-size label from card stock; use fabric glue to adhere to a piece from the tablecloth, then cut tablecloth piece one-inch larger on all sides than label.

6. Use marker to draw and pencils to color desired message on label.

7. Use fabric glue to adhere label to front of album. Tie floss into a bow at front of buttons, then glue one button at each corner of label…glue more buttons on front of album as desired.

PERSONALIZED PRESENT BASKETS

(shown on page 10)

Allow primer, paint and sealer to dry after each application.

Apply primer to the rim and handle of a large basket. Paint a checkerboard stripe around the rim, then paint the handle solid using one of the colors in the checkerboard. Apply two coats of sealer to the painted areas.

Refer to *Making A Tag Or Label*, page 130, to make a tag using card stock, fabric and corrugated craft cardboard…hot glue buttons at corners of tag, then glue to front of basket.

SNOWMAN CHAIR

(shown on page 11)

- drill and ¼" dia. bits
- child-size wooden chair with uprights
- wood glue
- two 2¾" long pieces of ¼" dia. wooden dowel
- two each 1½" dia. and 1¾" dia. wooden balls
- four 1½" dia. wooden rings
- sandpaper & tack cloth
- spray primer
- assorted colors of acrylic paint, including white, orange and pink
- paintbrushes
- black permanent fine-point marker
- clear acrylic spray sealer
- two toddler-size socks
- embroidery floss

Refer to Painting Techniques, page 130, for some tips from your Country Friends® before beginning project. Allow glue, primer, paint and sealer to dry after each application.

1. Drill a ½" deep hole at top center of each upright; glue dowels in holes. Drill a hole through center of each wooden ball.

2. For each snowmen finial, place two wooden rings, 1¾" diameter ball, then 1½" diameter ball on dowel; glue pieces to secure. Trim and sand dowel if necessary.

3. Apply primer to chair. Paint finials white and remaining sections of chair desired *Base Coat* colors.

4. Paint lights around the chair legs and uprights; paint a "socket" at wide end of each bulb, then paint an "electric cord" to connect the bulbs.

5. Paint white snowman heads on seat. Paint orange noses and pink cheeks on each snowman, including the finials. Use marker to draw eyes and a mouth on each snowman.

6. Paint a checkerboard along top and bottom edges of chair back slats. Paint child's name on top slat; paint white dots and snowflakes on bottom slat and around snowmen on seat.

7. Apply two coats of sealer to chair.

8. For each snowman hat, cut cuff from socks and fold finished edge of cuff up, then glue hat on snowman. Tie floss around hat close to head; trim end to desired length. Cut fringes in end of hat. For the scarf, cut a ¹/₂"w strip from remaining sock piece, then knot around the snowman's neck.

DECOUPAGED CLOCK
(shown on page 12)

"Turn back the hands of time" to your favorite memories from Christmases past. Stain a round wooden plaque to the desired color and allow it to dry. Sizing to fit your plaque, make a color photocopy of the clock face pattern from page 131 on heavy paper, then cut out. Glue the clock face onto the plaque and allow it to dry. Cut a Christmas motif from a card or paper and glue it to the clock face; lightly spray the clock with woodtone spray. Draw over the minute marks and circle with a broad black marker. Allowing to dry after each application, apply 2 to 3 coats of clear acrylic sealer to the plaque. Follow manufacturer's instructions to attach a clock kit to the plaque.

FAVORITE FOOD PHOTO LABELS
(shown on page 13)

Family favorite recipes seem even better in jars bearing photos of the prize cooks. Photocopy the labels on page 134. Use colored pencils to color them in, then glue on the photo. Glue or use double-stick tape to secure the label to a jar. Make a few for Aunt Betty…maybe she'll get the hint and bring a jar full of her Aunt Betty's best when she visits!

MEASURING CUP PHOTO HOLDER
(shown on page 15)

Turn Grandma's old measuring cup into a new picture holder to display some of the "immeasurable loves" in your life. Cut a piece of plastic foam to fit snugly in the measuring cup; glue in place. Overlapping ends at handle, glue jumbo rick-rack, then baby rick-rack around the cup…glue a big button at the front. For each picture holder, shape one end of a length of 20-gauge wire into a tight, flat coil; insert the uncoiled end into the cup. If desired, glue buttons to the centers of some of the coils. Finish by gluing lots of buttons over the foam.

SNOWCAPPED SAP BUCKETS
(shown on pages 16 and 17)

Lightly paint a sap bucket…you want some of the metal to show through the paint. Make a color copy of your favorite snowman image from pages 132 or 133; resize the image to fit your bucket if you want to. Cut out the image and glue it to the bucket. Now, the fun part! Apply a drift of snow medium around the top of the bucket…make a few falling flakes and random dots of white paint around the image while you're at it. Then, while the snow is still wet, sprinkle with glitter flakes.

NATURAL ORNAMENTS
(shown on page 22)

Bring the beauty of nature indoors… along with your evergreen…for the holiday season. Decorate small grapevine wreaths by wrapping berry garlands around the wreath and adding a bright raffia bow. Glue Spanish moss and eucalyptus leaves and berries in a gourd bell cup. Nestle several of these ornaments, along with a miniature faux bird's nest, among the branches of your tree…a bird nest is said to bring good luck and fortune by having been blessed by God's messengers…the birds!

HEARTS AFGHAN
(shown on page 30)

Refer to Crochet, page 128, for abbreviations and general instructions. When following chart, page 136, on right side rows, follow Chart from right to left; on wrong side rows, follow Chart from left to right.

Finished Size: Approximately 49"x61"

MATERIALS
Worsted Weight Yarn, approximately:
31 ounces, (880 grams or 2,125 yards)
Crochet hook, size I (5.50 mm) **or** size needed for gauge

GAUGE SWATCH: 10³/₄"w x 5¹/₄"h
Ch 45 **loosely.**
Work same as Afghan for 10 rows.
Finish off.

BASIC CHART STITCHES
Beginning Block over Block: Ch 3 **(counts as first dc)**, turn; dc in next 3 dc.

Ending Block over Block: Dc in last 3 dc.
Block over Block: Dc in next 3 dc.
Block over Space: 2 Dc in next ch-2 sp, dc in next dc.
Space over Space: Ch 2, dc in next dc.
Space over Block: Ch 2, skip next 2 dc, dc in next dc.

Note: Each row is worked across length of afghan.

Ch 240 **loosely.**

Row 1 (Wrong side): Dc in fourth ch from hook **(3 skipped chs count as first dc)** and in next 2 chs, ★ ch 2, skip next 2 chs, (dc in next ch, ch 2, skip next 2 chs) 11 times, dc in next 4 chs; repeat from ★ across: 94 dc and 72 ch-2 sps.

Rows 2-91: Follow Chart, page 136; do **not** finish off.

Edging: Ch 1, turn; (slip st, ch 2, dc) twice in first dc, skip next 2 dc, [[(slip st, ch 2, dc) in next 13 dc, skip next 2 dc] 6 times, (slip st, ch 2, dc, slip st) in last dc, ch 2; working in end of rows, skip first row, (slip st in next row, ch 2); working in free loops of beginning ch, (slip st, ch 2, dc) twice in first ch, skip next 2 chs, ★ (slip st, ch 2, dc) in next ch, skip next 2 chs; repeat from ★ 77 times **more**, (slip st, ch 2, dc, slip st) in last ch, ch 2; working in end of rows, slip st in first row, ch 2, (slip st in next row, ch 2) across to last row, skip last row; join with slip st to first slip st, finish off.

CROSS-STITCHED SAMPLER
(shown on page 31)

- embroidery floss (see color key for design, page 137)
- 8-inch sq. of white 14-ct Aida
- wooden frame to accommodate an 8"x10" mat
- old candle
- brown and ivory acrylic paint
- paintbrushes
- sandpaper
- tack cloth
- clear acrylic matte spray sealer
- 8"x10" red mat with 5¹/₂"w x 5³/₄"h opening centered 1³/₄" inches from top of mat
- hot glue gun
- one **Key Ornament** from page 32 with green ribbon

(continued on page 122)

Refer to Cross Stitch, page 128, before beginning project. Allow paint and sealer to dry after each application.

1. Using 2 strands of floss for Cross Stitches and one strand of floss for Backstitches, center and stitch design from page 137 on Aida.

2. Paint frame brown. Rub a candle randomly on frame, then paint frame ivory. Lightly sand frame over waxed areas for an aged look; wipe with tack cloth, then apply two coats of sealer to the frame.

3. Have stitched piece mounted in frame using red mat. Glue **Key Ornament** to mat.

MINI-SAMPLER ORNAMENT
(shown on page 32)

- embroidery floss (see color key for design, page 138)
- two 5-inch squares of white 16 ct. Aida
- polyester fiberfill
- tracing paper
- red felt

Refer to Cross Stitch, page 128, and Embroidery Stitches, page 129, before beginning project.

1. Using 2 strands of floss for Cross Stitches and one strand of floss for Backstitches, center and stitch design from page 138 on one piece of Aida.

2. Pin stitched piece to remaining Aida piece. Centering design 1/2" from bottom edge, draw a 3" wide x 4" high box around design; cut out along lines. Matching right sides and raw edges and leaving top open, sew pieces together 1/4" from edges. Turn ornament right-side out and lightly stuff with fiberfill.

3. Trace roof and chimney patterns, page 138, onto tracing paper. Use patterns to cut one chimney and two roof pieces from felt.

4. Pin top of stitched piece between scalloped edges of roof pieces; pin chimney in place between roof layers. Work a French Knot through each scallop along bottom of roof; work Running Stitches along top edges of roof.

HEART TREE SKIRT
(shown on page 33)

- freezer paper
- ecru and red felt for hearts
- pinking shears
- small, very sharp scissors
- 2 yards of 72" wide red felt for skirt
- string
- fabric marking pencil
- thumbtack
- 1 1/3 yards green fabric
- ecru lace trim

Use a 1/4" seam allowance for all sewing unless otherwise indicated.

1. Follow Steps 1 through 3 of **Felt Heart Ornaments**, page 32, to make 16 hearts.

2. Matching right sides, fold red felt for skirt in half from top to bottom and again from left to right.

3. Tie one end of string to pencil. Insert thumbtack through string 26-inches from the pencil. Insert thumbtack through the felt as shown in Fig. 1; mark the outside cutting line.

Fig. 1

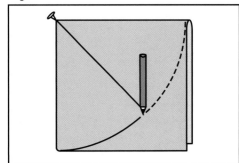

4. Repeat Step 3, inserting thumbtack 3 1/2" from the pencil; mark the inner cutting line. Cut along drawn lines through all layers of felt. Unfold and place skirt on a flat surface; draw a straight line from inner circle to outer edge...cut skirt open along line.

5. Piecing as necessary, cut a 4"x5 1/2" yd. bias strip from green fabric for trim. Matching wrong sides, press strip in half lengthwise.

6. Beginning and ending 1/2" past opening edges and matching raw edges, pin strip to right side of skirt along outer edge of circle; sew in place. Press trim flat. Press ends of trim 1/4" to wrong side, then 1/4" to wrong side again; sew in place.

7. For inner circle trim, unfold remaining bias strip. Press long edges of strip to center fold. Refold strip. Beginning and ending 1/2" past opening edges, pin edge of inner circle between fold of strip. Press ends of trim 1/4" to wrong side, then 1/4" to wrong side again; sew trim in place. Stitch lace to skirt over trim seams.

8. Spacing evenly, stitch hearts to skirt.

PAINTED CANDLEHOLDERS
(shown on page 35)

Allow paint to dry after each application.

Use a star-shaped sponge to Sponge Paint, page 130, yellow stars around a clear glass votive. Use a black paint pen to draw "stitches" along the edges of the stars and swirls coming off some of the stars.

Adhere evenly spaced strips of narrow masking tape around a tall glass votive...paint exposed areas red, then remove the tape.

Use a white paint pen to draw snowflakes around the rim of a flowerpot-shaped clear glass votive...add random-sized dots around the snowflakes.

Paint a round votive holder white like a snowman...use paint pens to add the nose and mouth. Glue on small shank buttons for eyes, then glue a torn strip of homespun around his "neck" for a muffler.

SNOWMAN PILLOW
(shown on page 40)

Make one of these happy snowman pillows to snuggle up with for a long winter's nap! Cut two 16" diameter circles from muslin. Trace the face pattern from page 142 onto tracing paper, then use transfer paper to transfer the design to the center of one of the circles...use paint pens to color the nose orange and the eyes and big smile black. Matching right sides and leaving an opening for turning, sew the circles together 1/4" from edges, then turn the pillow right-side out. Stuff pillow with polyester fiberfill and sew the opening closed.

SANTA WALL HANGING
(shown on pages 42 and 43)

- tissue paper
- white fabric
- red and white embroidery floss
- assorted red and red & white print fabrics for sashings and borders
- 20"x22" piece of fabric for backing
- 20"x22" piece of polyester batting
- assorted white buttons

Referring to Embroidery Stitches, page 129, work stitching through tissue paper patterns, then carefully tear away patterns. Match right sides and raw edges and use a 1/4" seam allowance for all sewing.

1. Trace Santa design, page 144, onto tissue paper; pin pattern to the center of a 9 1/2"x11 1/2" piece of white fabric. Use 3 strands of red floss and an *Outline Stitch* to stitch the design.

2. For wall hanging top, cut two 1 3/4"x9 1/2" top/bottom sashing strips and two 1 3/4"x14" side sashing strips from red fabric. Sew top and bottom, then side strips to stitched piece.

3. Cut 3" long pieces from red fabrics in varying widths from 1 3/4" to 2 1/2". Sew pieces together to make two 12" long top/bottom borders and two 19" long side borders. Sew top and bottom, then side borders to wall hanging top.

4. Matching dashed lines and arrows, trace word patterns, page 144, onto tissue paper 4 times; pin patterns along sashings. Use 2 strands of white floss and an *Outline Stitch* to stitch words.

5. Place backing fabric, wrong-side up, on a flat surface. Smooth batting on backing, then center wall hanging top, right-side up, on batting; pin layers together. Sew layers together by stitching along the inner and outer seams of the sashings.

6. For hanging sleeve, cut a 7"x15" strip from fabric. Press ends 1/4" to wrong side, press 1/4" to wrong side again and sew in place. Matching wrong sides and long edges, press strip in half. Matching raw edges, baste hanging sleeve to top edge on back of wall hanging.

7. Cut two 2 1/2"x20" top/bottom and two 2 1/2"x22" side binding strips from fabric. Matching wrong sides and long edges, press each strip in half. Matching raw edges, sew top and bottom bindings to wall hanging. Trim backing and batting from top and bottom edges 1/4" larger than wall hanging top. Trim binding ends even with edges of wall hanging top. Fold bindings over to backing, covering stitch lines, and hand stitch in place.

8. Center and sew side bindings to wall hanging. Trim backing and batting 1/4" larger than wall hanging top. Trim each end of binding 1/2" longer than bound wall hanging. Fold each end of binding over to backing; pin in place. Fold bindings over to backing, covering stitch lines, and hand stitch in place.

9. Hand stitch bottom of hanging sleeve to back of wall hanging. Tying floss into a bow at front of buttons, use floss to sew buttons randomly to quilt.

PEEKING SANTA WINDOW
(shown on page 47)

Use an almost square, to-good-to-toss, old wooden-frame window for this project. Clean the glass, then wipe both sides with alcohol and allow it to dry.

To determine size of the squares needed for your drawing grid, divide the width of your window by 8. Working on the front side of the glass, use a grease pencil to mark center lines down and across window, then draw the grid 8 squares high and 8 squares wide. Referring to the Santa pattern, page 141, use the grease pencil to draw the design on the front side of the window.

Working on the back side of the glass and allowing paints to dry after each application, use a broad-point black paint pen to draw over Santa, moon and snow lines and a white paint pen to draw snowflakes. Paint cheeks, then use desired colors of acrylic paint to complete the painting. Clean the grease pencil from the glass.

Cut a piece of heavy-duty cardboard to fit in the window; cut a piece of snowflake-print fabric one inch larger on all sides than the cardboard piece. Wrapping the edges to the back, glue the fabric to the cardboard; place in frame behind painting and glue to secure.

COOKIE PULL TOYS
(shown on pages 48 and 49)

Enchant the little ones with these whimsical gingerbread "toy" treats...fun to make, and even more fun to eat!

Important! Use 1/2 teaspoon of baking soda instead of 1 teaspoon when making the cookie dough and roll out the dough to 1/4" thick before cutting out shapes.

Following the recipe for Great Grandma's Christmas Cookies on page 118, use jumbo animal cookie cutters to make two shapes alike for each pull toy (remember to flip one over before you bake them).

For our Royal icing "glue", mix 3 tablespoons meringue powder, 4 cups powdered sugar and 6 tablespoons warm water together in a medium bowl. Beat with an electric mixer for 7 to 10 minutes until stiff...this will make 3 cups of icing.

For each pull toy, use paste food coloring to color icing the desired color; ice the "outsides" of one pair of cookies, add sprinkles or allow the icing to harden, then add details using a cake decorator's bag with a small round tip and white icing.

Glue 2 vanilla wafers between cookies for a spacer...be sure to glue the cookies evenly so that the animal will stand.

For each "wagon", glue 2 full-size graham crackers together...place one end of a piece of red string licorice between layers for the "pull rope." Glue vanilla wafer "wheels" to the wagon, then one chocolate-covered candy piece to the center of each wheel.

Center and glue your animal on the wagon...now you're ready for a parade that any child, young or old, will delight in!

PUPILS' GIFT BAGS

(shown on page 57)

- 1/4" wide paper-backed fusible tape
- homespun
- spray primer
- yellow and dark yellow acrylic paint
- paintbrushes
- wooden star cut-outs
- black and red permanent fine-point markers
- clear acrylic spray sealer
- coordinating color of raffia
- hot glue gun

Allow primer, paint and sealer to dry after each application.

1. For each bag, cut two 5" lengths of fusible tape and one 5"x15" piece of homespun. Fuse one length of tape to wrong side of each short end of homespun; do not remove paper backing. Press each end 1/4" to the wrong side, remove paper backing and press to secure. Matching ends and right sides, fold fabric piece in half and stitch raw edges together; turn bag right-side out.

2. For tag, apply primer, then two coats yellow paint to star cut-out. *Dry Brush, page 130,* tag with dark yellow paint. Use black marker to write message and draw swirls and dots on tag; use red marker to draw small stars on tag. Apply 2 coats of sealer to tag.

3. Place a gift in the bag, then use raffia to tie bag closed. Glue tag to knot in raffia.

HEART BASKET

(shown on page 57)

Allow paint and sealer to dry after each application.

Applying one light coat of paint, painting in one direction only and allowing paint to streak, paint wooden heart cut-outs red. Apply sealer to hearts. Hot glue hearts around outside of basket.

Line the basket with a piece of fabric… you can hem or fringe the edges if you'd like.

Refer to Making A Tag Or Label, page 130, to make a tag for your gift.

SEWING GIFT BASKET

(shown on page 56 and 57)

Every seamstress you know would be "in stitches" to receive this unique gift basket! Find a basket with built-in compartments and a sturdy handle for ease in carrying; hot glue assorted colors of buttons around the rim of the basket. Make a handy pincushion by gluing a 9" diameter circle of fabric around a 3" diameter plastic foam ball, stretching and smoothing fabric to the bottom of the ball as you glue. Place the pincushion in one of the compartments, then fill the remaining compartments with assorted sewing items…a tape measure, scissors, fat-quarters of assorted fabrics and maybe a few quilter's pins. For a "fitting" tag, photocopy the tag design from page 156 onto white card stock, then glue the tag onto a coordinating color of card stock…use decorative-edge craft scissors to trim the card stock edges 1/4" larger on all sides than the tag. Punch a hole in the tag and thread the tag and several assorted-shaped buttons onto a piece of craft wire and attach to the handle of the basket. For an extra special touch, add a batch of mouth-watering button-shaped cookies baked fresh the morning you present your gift.

PENNY RUG STOCKING ORNAMENT

(shown on page 60)

- tracing paper
- red, black and gold felt
- pinking shears
- black, gold and green embroidery floss
- wooden buttons

Refer to Embroidery Stitches, page 129, before beginning project. Use 3 strands of floss for all stitching. Refer to pattern for "penny" and "snowflake" placement.

1. Trace mini stocking and small and large circle patterns, page 146, onto tissue paper. Pin stocking pattern to red felt and cut out along pattern lines for stocking front. Remove pattern and pin to black felt; use pinking shears to cut out stocking back 1/4" outside pattern lines.

2. Using large circle pattern and pinking shears, cut 3 circles from gold felt; use small circle pattern to cut out 3 red circles. For each penny, stack a large circle, then a small circle on stocking front; use black floss to sew a button through all layers at center of stack to secure in place. Work black *Running Stitches* 1/8" outside gold circle and gold *Blanket Stitches* along edges of red circles.

3. For each snowflake, use gold floss to work *Straight Stitches* for snowflake points and a *French Knot* at center of points. Work green *French Knots* randomly on stocking.

4. Pin stocking front to stocking back; leaving top edge open, work *Blanket Stitches* along stocking front edges to sew pieces together.

5. For the hanger, cut a 1/2"x9" strip of felt, fold in half and stitch ends between layers at heel-side of stocking.

TREE STOCKINGS

(shown on page 61)

- red and gold felt for stockings
- pinking shears
- green, brown, gold and assorted colors of felt
- paper-backed fusible web
- gold embroidery floss
- assorted buttons

Refer to Embroidery Stitches, page 129, before beginning project. Use 3 strands of floss for all stitching.

1. Use a copy machine to enlarge the stocking patterns on page 147 by 200%. For each stocking, pin pattern to one color of felt for stocking and cut out along pattern lines for stocking front. Remove pattern and pin to remaining color of felt for stocking; use pinking shears to cut out stocking back 1/4" outside pattern lines.

2. Using enlarged patterns, trace tree, trunk and star patterns onto paper side of web. Fuse tree to green felt, trunk to brown felt, star to gold felt and pieces of web to assorted colors of felt for "ornaments." Cut out tree, trunk and star appliqués. Use pinking shears to cut assorted sizes of circles for ornaments.

3. Arrange and fuse appliqués on stocking front; use floss to work *Blanket Stitches* along edges of trunk, tree, star and desired ornaments. Sew buttons to the center of some of the ornaments and to the star...sew a few buttons here and there on the tree.

4. Pin stocking front to stocking back; leaving top edge open, work *Blanket Stitches* along stocking front edges to sew pieces together.

5. For the hanger, cut one 1"x8" bottom strip from felt, then use pinking shears to cut one ³/4"x8" top strip from a different color of felt. Center top strip on bottom strip; work *Blanket Stitches* along long edges of top strip. Matching short ends, fold hanger in half.

6. For cuff, use pinking shears to cut a 5"x14" strip from felt. Using a ¹/2" seam allowance, sew short ends together; turn right-side out. Matching cuff seam to heel seam in stocking and matching top of stocking with one edge of cuff, place cuff in stocking. Matching raw edges, place hanger at heel seam between cuff and stocking layers. Sew cuff to stocking. Fold cuff 3" to outside of stocking. Work *Blanket Stitches* along edge of cuff.

HIS & HERS SLIPPERS
(shown on page 66)

Warm hearts and cozy feet...the perfect combination for any Christmas season! Just purchase snugly-soft house slippers and embellish with sewn-on seasonal motifs...use the patterns from page 146 and refer to *Embroidery Stitches*, page 129, for stitching tips from your Country Friends©.

For his slippers, trace the reindeer pattern onto tracing paper. Using the pattern, cut 2 reindeer (one in reverse) from brown shaggy felt. Arrange, then stitch the shapes on the shoes...use 6 strands of brown embroidery floss to make a *French Knot* nose and eyes and to *Backstitch* the antlers...work *Running Stitches* along slipper tops. Sew a few star-shaped buttons on the slippers.

For her slippers, trace the heart pattern onto tracing paper; use the pattern to cut two hearts from gold felt. Use 6 strands of black floss to *Blanket Stitch* the hearts on the shoes. Use 3 strands of green floss to *Backstitch* the evergreen branches around each heart; work a few *French Knot* red berries amid the branches. Sew a star-shaped button to the center of each heart.

GINGERBREAD DOLL
(shown on page 67)

DOLL
- paper-backed fusible web
- red fabric and brown felt
- tracing paper
- pinking shears
- white baby rick-rack
- white embroidery floss
- polyester fiberfill

Refer to Embroidery Stitches, page 129, before beginning project.

1. Trace the heart pattern, page 132, onto paper side of web; fuse to red fabric. Trace gingerbread pattern onto tracing paper. Using pattern and pinking shears, cut 2 gingerbread boys from brown felt, then cut out heart.

2. Fuse heart to one gingerbread boy. Sew pieces of rick-rack along arms and legs. Using 3 strands of floss, *Whip Stitch* along edges of heart and gingerbread boy; work *Running Stitches* for mouth and eyebrows and *Satin Stitches* for eyes, nose and cheeks.

3. Pin gingerbread boy pieces together; using 6 strands of floss and leaving an opening for stuffing, *Whip Stitch* edges together. Stuff doll with fiberfill and sew opening closed.

STUFFED SNOWMAN DOLL
(shown on page 68)

- orange and black felt
- white chenille fabric
- green and red polar fleece
- fabric glue
- polyester fiberfill
- black, green and red embroidery floss

Refer to Embroidery Stitches, page 129, and use 6 strands of floss for all embroidery. Match right sides and use a ¹/4" seam allowance for all sewing.

1. Use a photocopy machine to enlarge the snowman patterns on page 150 and 151 by 200%. Using the patterns, cut one nose from orange felt, 2 bodies and 4 arms from chenille and 4 large circles and 7 small circles from black felt. Cut one 2"x27" piece for scarf and one 3"x12" piece for pom-pom from green fleece and one 13" square hat from red fleece.

2. On the right side of one body piece, arrange the large circles for eyes and buttons, the small circles for a mouth and the nose. Glue mouth pieces in place; allow to dry. Using black floss, work a *Cross Stitch* through each eye and button. Using orange floss, work *Running Stitches* along short edge of nose.

3. For each arm, sew 2 arm pieces together; turn right-side out. Leaving ¹/2" at top for seam allowance, stuff with fiberfill. Referring to Fig. 1, pin arms to snowman front; baste in place.

Fig. 1

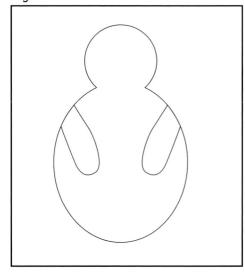

4. Leaving an opening for turning, sew body pieces together, then turn right-side out. Stuff doll with fiberfill and sew opening closed.

5. Fold hat piece in half. Referring to Fig. 2 on page 126, mark hat piece diagonally; sew along mark and trim seam allowance to ¹/4". Work *Running Stitches* around narrow end of hat; pull thread to gather and tie to secure. Turn hat right-side out; work green *Blanket Stitches* along bottom edge.

continued on page 126

Fig. 2

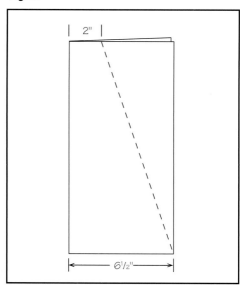

6. Using pattern, cut 4 mitten pieces from red fleece. For each mitten, place 2 mitten pieces together. Leaving cuff open, work green *Blanket Stitches* along mitten edges, then around cuff opening. Place mittens on arms and tack in place.

7. For pom-pom, work *Running Stitches* down center of pom-pom piece. Make clips along long edges just short of stitches. Pull thread ends to gather; knot thread tightly around gathers to secure. Tack pom-pom to tip of hat; place hat on snowman.

8. Make clips along short ends of scarf for fringe. Work red *Blanket Stitches* along long edges and *Cross Stitches* above fringes on scarf...wrap scarf around snowman's neck.

MOLLOHAN'S MIX JAR
(shown on page 74)

- spray primer
- red spray paint
- one pint wide-mouth canning jar
- fabric scraps
- cardboard
- high-loft polyester batting
- coordinating heavy-duty thread
- embroidery floss
- button with holes
- hot glue gun
- raffia
- acrylic paint
- paintbrushes
- wooden star cut-out
- black permanent fine-point marker

1. Allowing primer and paint to dry after each coat, apply primer, then 2 coats of red paint to jar lid ring.

2. To make yo-yo, cut one 7" diameter circle of fabric, one 3" diameter circle of cardboard and three 3" diameter circles of batting. Press raw edges of fabric circle 1/4" to the wrong side; using heavy-duty thread, work loose *Running Stitches*, page 129, along pressed edge. Place fabric circle, wrong-side up, on a flat surface; place cardboard circle, then batting circles at center of fabric circle. Pull ends of thread to tightly gather fabric circle over batting circles; knot thread ends to secure. With knot on bottom, tie floss through holes in button; glue button over gathers of yo-yo. Glue flat side of yo-yo to top of lid.

3. Tear one wide and one narrow strip of fabric to fit around jar. Overlapping ends at back of jar, glue wide strip, then narrow strip around jar. Tie several strands of raffia into a bow around center of jar.

4. Refer to *Painting Techniques*, page 130, to paint the star cut-out. Use marker to write message on star; glue star to bow.

PAINTED SNOWMAN TIN
(shown on page 75)

- tin with lid
- spray primer
- red, green, black and white acrylic paint
- paintbrushes
- textured snow medium
- black, orange and white paint pens

Paint outside of tin and lid only. Allow primer, paint and snow medium to dry after each application.

1. Spray lid and tin with primer. Paint top of lid red. Leaving a 1/2" wide strip around bottom of tin, paint tin green. Paint a black & white checkerboard around side of lid and bottom of tin.

2. Use snow medium to paint snowman heads. Use paint pens to draw black eyes and mouths and an orange nose on each head; draw a few white "snowflakes" and dots on tin.

CRACKER WRAPS
(shown on page 77)

Center a piece of wax paper on the wrong side of a piece of decorative tissue paper. Lay a stack of crackers down the center of the wax paper; gently roll the paper

around crackers and twist ends. Tie rick-rack around the ends to secure.

ORIENTAL SAUCE BOTTLE
(shown on page 78)

To seal bottle, melt desired color of candle wax in a clean can placed in 2" of boiling water in an electric skillet. Dip top of bottle, past lid or cork, into wax, then remove and allow to cool. Repeat process until desired thickness of wax covers lid or cork. Knot a few strands of raffia around waxed top.

For the tag, photocopy the tag design, page 156, onto ecru card stock. Refer to *Making A Tag Or Label*, page 130, to complete tag. Punch a 1/8" diameter hole in corner of tag; use raffia to attach tag and a pair of chopsticks to the bottle.

Wrap the center of an 8-inch length of small rusted star garland around the chopsticks; twist the ends of the garland into curls.

APPLE BUCKLE ENSEMBLE
(shown on page 84)

- fabric
- jumbo rick-rack
- 13"x9" baking dish
- clear cellophane
- raffia
- wooden mixing spoon
- craft glue
- white card stock
- decorative-edge craft scissors
- photocopy of recipe (page 151) on white card stock
- 4 buttons

1. For topping bag, matching wrong sides and short edges, fold a 5"x14" piece of fabric in half; sew sides of bag together, then turn right-side out. Place the topping mix in the bag and use rick-rack to tie the bag closed.

2. Place baking dish at center of a 36-inch square of cellophane. Place bag and 2 cans of apple pie filling in baking dish. Gather cellophane over dish; tie several lengths of raffia into a bow around gathers and a wooden mixing spoon.

3. For recipe card, cut a 3"x5" piece of fabric; glue to white card stock, then use craft scissors to trim edges 1/8-inch outside fabric edges. Cut out and glue photocopied recipe to fabric-covered card. Glue rick-rack along edges of recipe; glue one button to each corner of rick-rack.

SAVORY BUTTERS BASKET
(shown on page 79)

Beginning at the center front of a cracker basket, weave grosgrain ribbon through the holes on the sides of the basket; hot glue ribbon ends to secure. Tie a length of ribbon into a bow, then glue a button to the knot. Glue sprigs of greenery, then the bow to the front of the basket over the ribbon ends.

Overlapping ends at front, wrap and glue a length of ribbon around each jar. For jar labels, copy the label designs from page 155 onto card stock. Color the stars yellow, then cut out the labels. Glue a label to the front of each jar.

SNOWMAN MUG AND BAG
(shown on page 80)

For each snowman mug, use paint pens to draw "coal" eyes, a big smile and an orange carrot nose on a white microwave-safe coffee mug.

Match the long edges and right sides of a 10"x15" torn piece of fabric; sew the long edges and one short end of fabric together, then turn bag right-side out. For the cake-mix-filled "hat," place a bag of mix and glaze in the fabric bag and tie closed with a satin ribbon. Place the bag in the mug.

Use the instructions in the recipe on page 80 and follow the Country Friends® Making A Tag Or Label instructions on page 130 to make the recipe card.

ONION SOUP MIX BAG
(shown on page 81)

- homespun
- photocopy of recipe cards (page 155) onto ecru card stock

1. For bag, tear a 6"x15" piece of homespun. Matching short edges and right sides, fold homespun piece in half; using a 1/2" seam allowance, sew sides of bag together, then turn right-side out.

2. Place mix in bag. Tie a strip torn from homespun into a bow around top of bag.

3. Using the photocopied recipe cards, refer to Making A Tag Or Label on page 130 to make a set of cards to give with your gift.

Sew up a stack of Santa hats for friends & family... use fuzzy, funny fabrics just to be silly! What fun!

An effort made for the happiness of others lifts us above ourselves.
~LYDIA CHILD~

GENERAL INSTRUCTIONS

CROCHET

ABBREVIATIONS

ch(s)	chain(s)
dc	double crochet(s)
mm	millimeters
sp(s)	space(s)
st(s)	stitch(es)
YO	yarn over

★ - work instructions following ★ as many **more** times as indicated in addition to the first time.

( ) or [ ] - work enclosed instructions **as many** times as specified by the number immediately following **or** work all enclosed instructions in the stitch or space indicated **or** contains explanatory remarks

colon (:) the number(s) given after a colon at the end of a row or round denote(s) the number of stitches you should have on that row or round.

Slip stitch (slip st): Insert hook in st or sp indicated. YO and draw through st or sp **and** through loop on hook (**Fig. 1**).

Fig. 1

Double crochet (dc): YO, insert hook in st or sp indicated, YO and pull up a loop (3 loops on hook), YO and draw through 2 loops on hook (**Fig. 2a**), YO and draw through remaining 2 loops on hook (**Fig. 2b**).

Fig. 2a

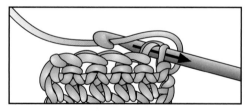

Fig. 2b

Free loops of a chain: When instructed to work in free loop of a chain, work in loop indicated by arrow (**Fig. 3**).

Fig. 3

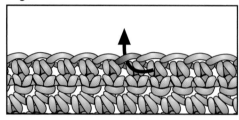

Finishing hints: Good finishing techniques make a big difference in the quality of the finished piece. Make a habit of weaving in loose ends as you work. To keep loose ends from showing, always weave them back through several stitches or work over them. When ends are secure, clip them off close to your work.

CROSS STITCH

Counted Cross Stitch (X): Work one Cross Stitch to correspond to each colored square in chart. For horizontal rows, work stitches in two journeys (**Fig. 1**).

Fig. 1

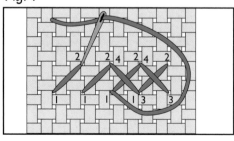

For vertical rows, complete stitch as shown (**Fig. 2**).

Fig. 2

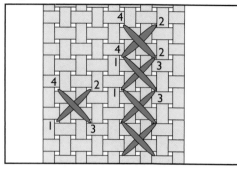

Backstitch (B'ST): For outline detail, Backstitch (shown in chart and color key by black or colored straight lines) should be worked after all Cross Stitch has been completed.

Fig. 3

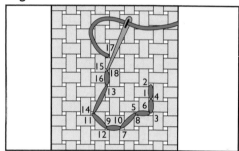

French Knot: Referring to Fig. 5, bring needle up at 1. Wrap floss once around needle and insert needle at 2, holding end of floss with non-stitching fingers.

Fig. 4

Quarter Stitch: Quarter Stitches are shown as triangular shapes of color in chart and color key. Come up at 1, then split fabric thread to take needle down at 2.

Fig. 5

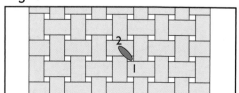

EMBROIDERY STITCHES

Preparing floss: If your project will be laundered, soak floss in a mixture of one cup water and one tablespoon vinegar for a few minutes and allow to dry before using to prevent colors from bleeding or fading.

Backstitch: Referring to Fig. 1, bring needle up at 1; go down at 2; bring up at 3 and pull through. For next stitch, insert needle at 1; bring up at 4 and pull through.

Fig. 1

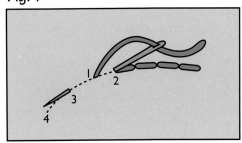

Blanket Stitch: Referring to Fig. 2a, bring needle up at 1. Keeping thread below point of needle, go down at 2 and come up at 3. Countine working as shown in Fig. 2b.

Fig. 2a

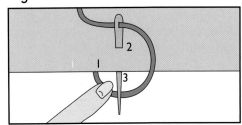

Fig. 2b

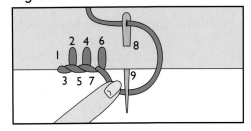

Cross Stitch: Bring needle up at 1 and go down at 2. Come up at 3 and go down at 4 (Fig. 3).

Fig. 3

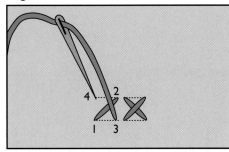

French Knot: Referring to Fig. 4, bring needle up at 1. Wrap floss once around needle and insert needle at 2, holding end of floss with non-stitching fingers. Tighten knot, then pull needle through fabric, holding floss until it must be released. For a larger knot, use more strands; wrap only once.

Fig. 4

Outline Stitch: Come up at 1. Keeping thread below the stitching line, go down at 2 and come up at 3. Go down at 4 and come up at 5 (Fig. 5).

Fig.5

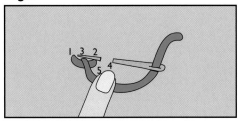

Running Stitch: Referring to Fig. 6, make a series of straight stitches with stitch length equal to the space between stitches.

Fig. 6

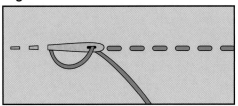

Satin Stitch: Referring to Fig. 7, come up at odd numbers and go down at even numbers with the stitches touching but not overlapping.

Fig. 7

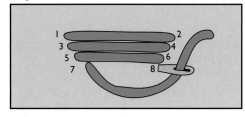

Straight Stitch: Referring to Fig. 8, come up at 1 and go down at 2.

Fig. 8

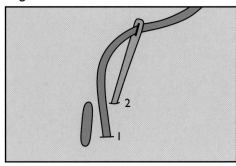

Whip Stitch: With right sides of folded fabric edges together, bring needle up at 1; take thread around edge of fabric and bring needle up at 2. Continue stitching along edge of fabric.

Fig. 9

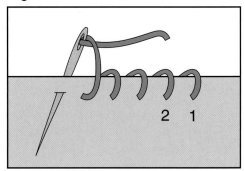

GENERAL INSTRUCTIONS (continued)

PAINTING TECHNIQUES

Transferring a pattern: Trace the pattern onto tracing paper. Place the transfer paper, coated-side down, between project and traced pattern. Use removable tape to secure the pattern to the project. Use a pencil to draw over the outlines of design (press lightly to avoid smudges and heavy lines that are difficult to cover). If necessary, use a soft eraser to remove any smudges.

Painting base coats: Use a medium round brush for large areas and a small round brush for small areas. Do not over-load brush. Allowing to dry between coats, apply several thin coats of paint to project.

Transferring details: To transfer detail lines to design, reposition pattern and transfer paper over painted base coats and use a pencil to lightly draw over detail lines of design.

Adding details: Use permanent marker or paint pen to draw over detail lines.

Dry Brush: Do not dip brush in water. Dip a stipple brush or old paintbrush in paint; wipe most of the paint off onto a dry paper towel. Lightly rub the brush across the area to receive color. Decrease pressure on the brush as you move outward. Repeat as needed.

Shading and highlighting: Dip one corner of a flat brush in water; blot on a paper towel. Dip dry corner of brush into paint. Stroke brush back and forth on palette until there is a gradual change from paint to water in each brush stroke. Stroke loaded side of brush along detail line on project, pulling brush toward you and turning project if necessary. For shading, side load brush with a darker color of paint. For highlighting, side load brush with a lighter color of paint.

Spatter Painting: Dip the bristle tips of a dry toothbrush into paint, blot on a paper towel to remove excess, then pull thumb across bristles to spatter paint on project.

Sponge Painting: Use an assembly-line method when making several sponge-painted projects. Place project on a covered work surface. Practice sponge-painting technique on scrap paper until desired look is achieved. Paint projects with first color and allow to dry before moving to next color. Use a clean sponge for each additional color.

For allover designs, dip dampened sponge piece into paint; remove excess paint on a paper towel. Use a light stamping motion to paint item.

For painting with sponge shapes, dip a dampened sponge shape into paint; remove excess paint on a paper towel. Lightly press sponge shape onto project. Carefully lift sponge. For a reverse design, turn sponge shape over.

MAKING PATTERNS

When the entire pattern is shown, place tracing paper over the pattern and draw over lines. For a more durable pattern, use a permanent marker to draw over pattern on stencil plastic.

When patterns are stacked or over-lapped, place tracing paper over the pattern and follow a single colored line to trace the pattern. Repeat to trace each pattern separately onto tracing paper.

When tracing a two-part pattern, match the dashed lines and arrows to trace the pattern onto tracing paper.

When only half of the pattern is shown (indicated by a solid blue line on pattern), fold the tracing paper in half. Place the fold along the solid blue line and trace pattern half; turn folded paper over and draw over the traced lines on the remaining side. Unfold the pattern; cut out.

MAKING A TAG OR LABEL

For a quick and easy tag or label, photocopy desired tag or label design onto card stock...or trace design onto tracing paper, then use transfer paper to transfer design to card stock. Color tag or label with colored pencils, crayons or thinned acrylic paint; draw over transferred lines using permanent markers or paint pens. Use straight-edge or decorative-edge craft scissors to cut out tag or label; glue to colored or decorative paper or card stock. Leaving a border around tag or label, cut tag from paper. Use a pen or marker to write a message on the tag or label.

MACHINE APPLIQUÉ

Unless otherwise indicated in project instructions, set sewing machine for a medium-width zigzag stitch with a short stitch length. When using nylon or metallic thread, use regular thread in bobbin.

1. Pin or baste a piece of stabilizer slightly larger than design to wrong side of background fabric under design.

2. Beginning on straight edge of appliqué if possible, position project under presser foot so that most of stitching will be on appliqué piece. Hold upper thread toward you and sew two or three stitches over thread to prevent raveling. Stitch over all exposed raw edges of appliqué and along detail lines as indicated in project instructions.

3. When stitching is complete, remove stabilizer. Pull loose threads to wrong side of fabric; knot and trim ends.

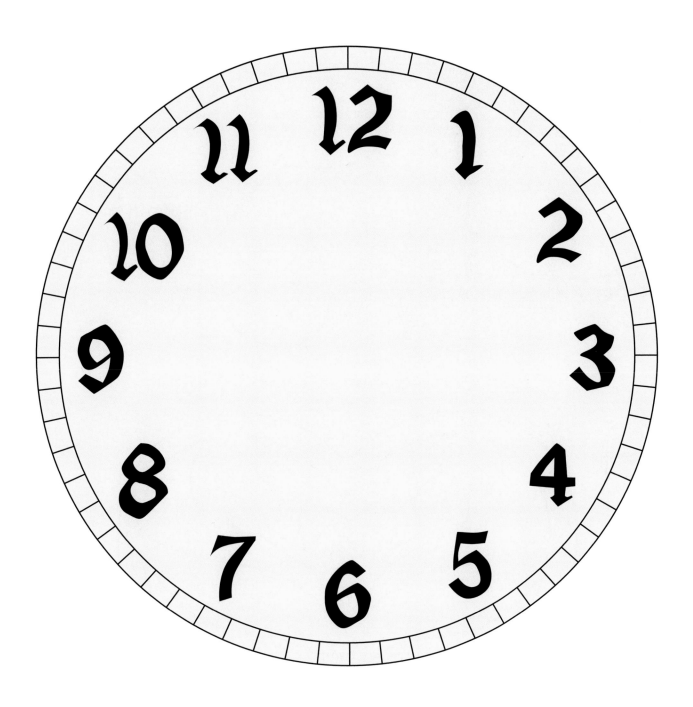

SNOWCAPPED SAP BUCKETS
(pages 16-17)

GINGERBREAD BOY BIB AND DOLL
(page 67)

FELT HEART ORNAMENT
(page 32)

Photo here

Photo here

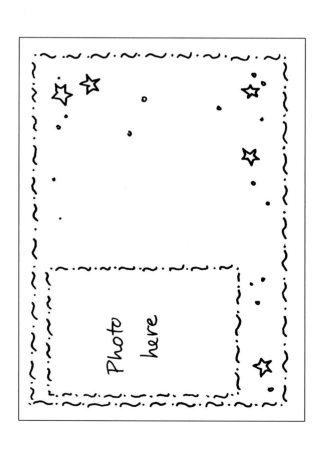

Photo here

welcome

Enlarge pattern 200%

CHRISTMAS LIGHTS WELCOME MAT
(pages 20-21)

SAP BUCKET ORNAMENTS
(page 19)

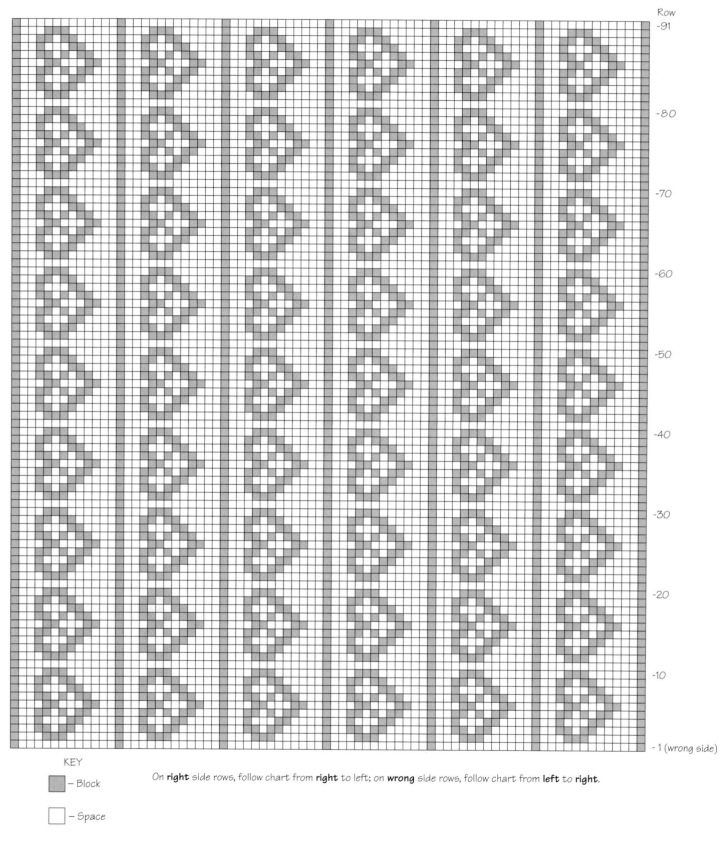

Row
-91

-80

-70

-60

-50

-40

-30

-20

-10

- 1 (wrong side)

KEY

☐ – Block

☐ – Space

On **right** side rows, follow chart from **right** to left; on **wrong** side rows, follow chart from **left** to **right**.

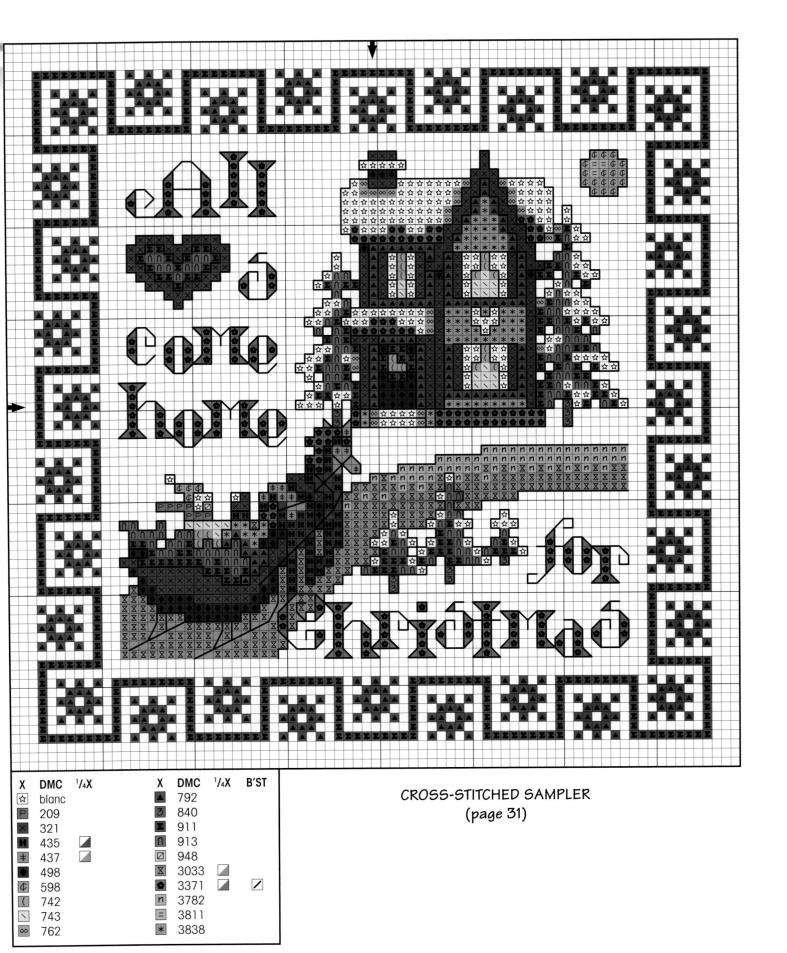

CROSS-STITCHED SAMPLER
(page 31)

X	DMC	¹/₄X		X	DMC	¹/₄X	B'ST
☆	blanc			▲	792		
P	209			3	840		
✕	321			Σ	911		
H	435	◢		∩	913		
‡	437	◢		⊘	948		
⬟	498			✕	3033	◢	
¢	598			⬠	3371	◢	╱
(	742			n	3782		
╲	743			=	3811		
∞	762			✳	3838		

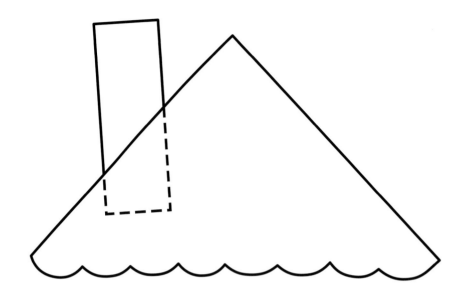

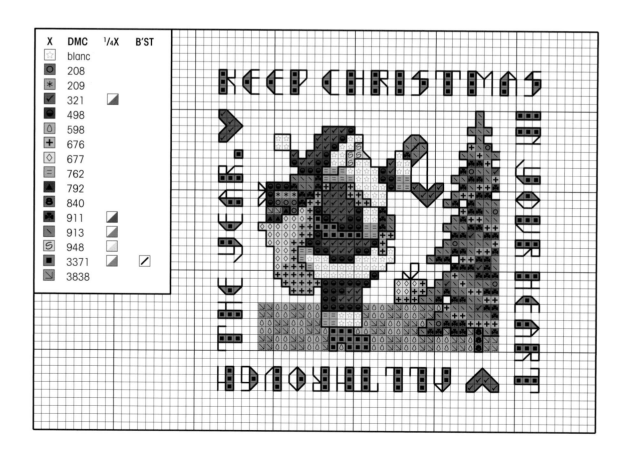

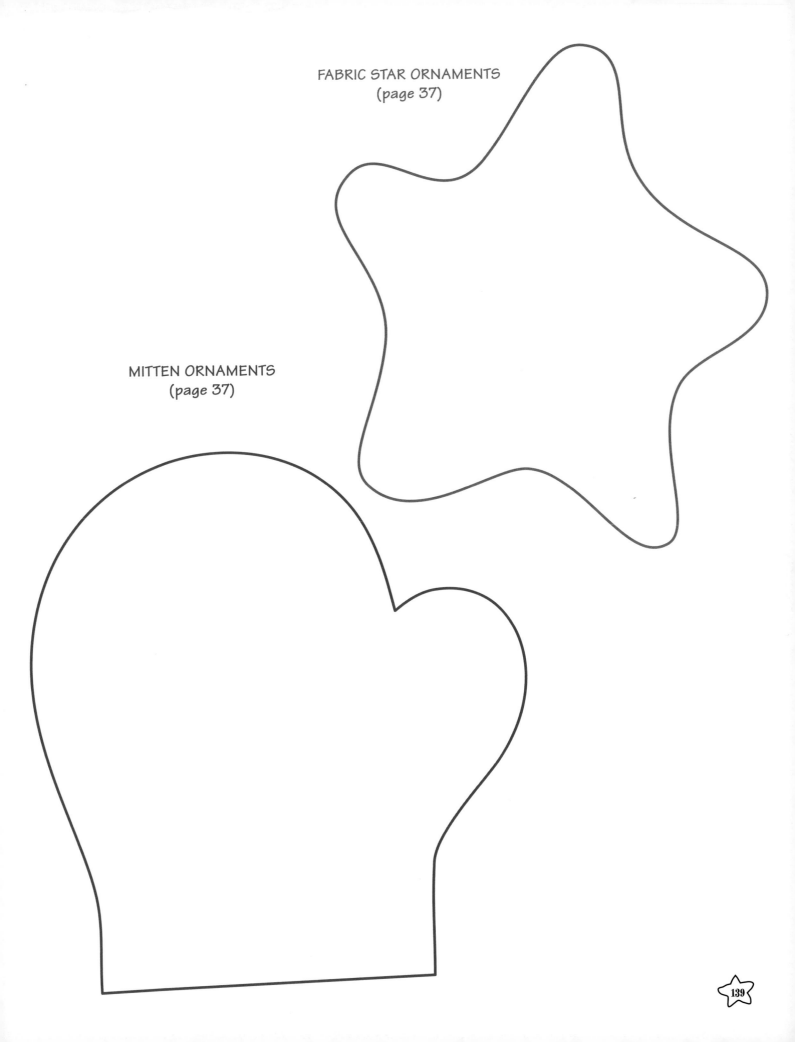

FABRIC STAR ORNAMENTS
(page 37)

MITTEN ORNAMENTS
(page 37)

139

MITTEN STOCKING OR PILLOWS
(pages 36 and 39)
Enlarge pattern 200%

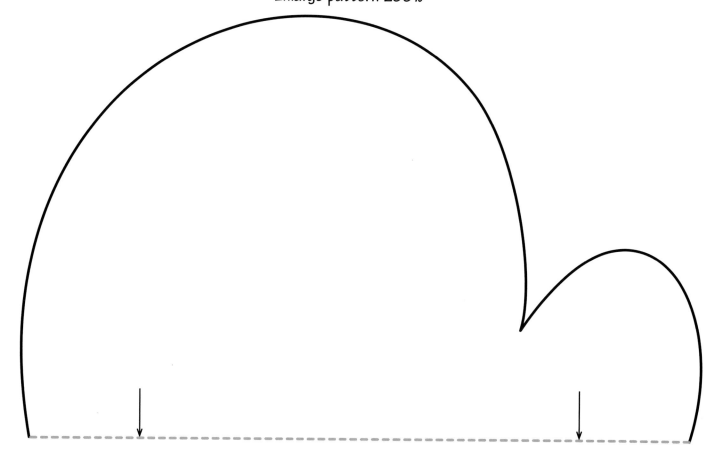

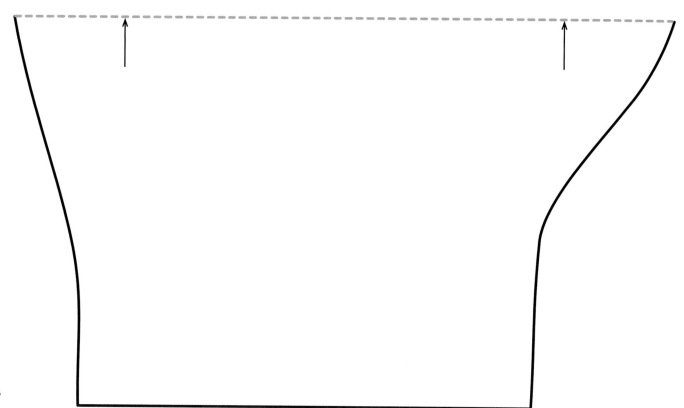

PATCHWORK COASTER
(page 64)

SANTA WALL HANGING
(pages 42-43)

joy ~ wishes ~ blessings ~ love

HIS & HERS SLIPPERS
(page 66)

PENNY RUG STOCKING ORNAMENT
(page 60)

TREE STOCKING
(page 61)
Enlarge pattern 200%

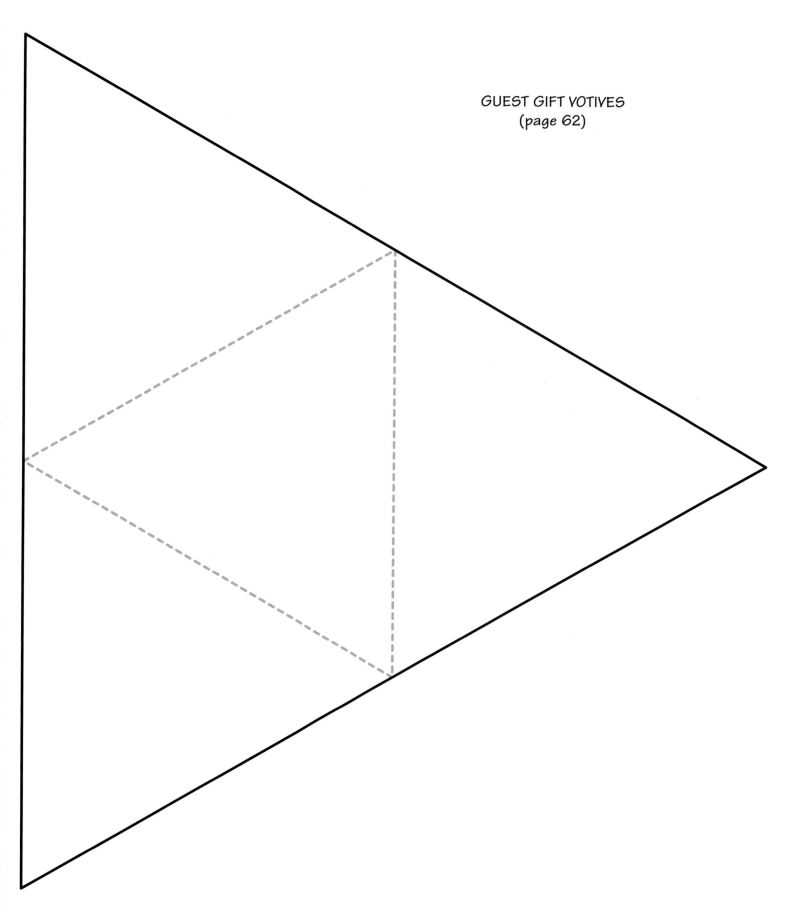

GUEST GIFT VOTIVES
(page 62)

148

NEEDLEPOINT "FRIENDS" PILLOW
(page 65)

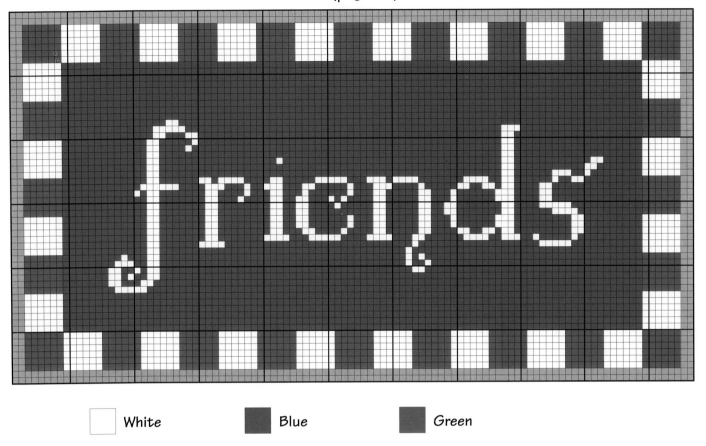

	White		Blue		Green

SNOWMAN ORNAMENTS
(page 37)

KIDS' HOLIDAY HATS
(page 67)

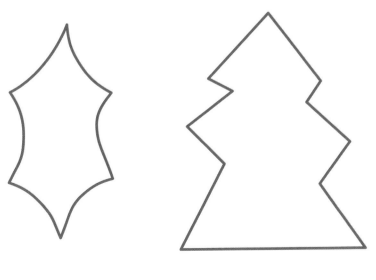

STUFFED SNOWMAN DOLL
(page 68)
Enlarge pattern 200%

STUFFED SNOWMAN DOLL
(page 68)
Enlarge pattern 200%

APPLE BUCKEL ENSEMBLE
(page 84)

Sweet Apple Buckle

Spread both cans of apple pie filling in a lightly oiled 13" x 9" baking pan. Sprinkle topping over apples and bake at 400 degrees for 20 minutes or until mixture bubbles.

Serves 12

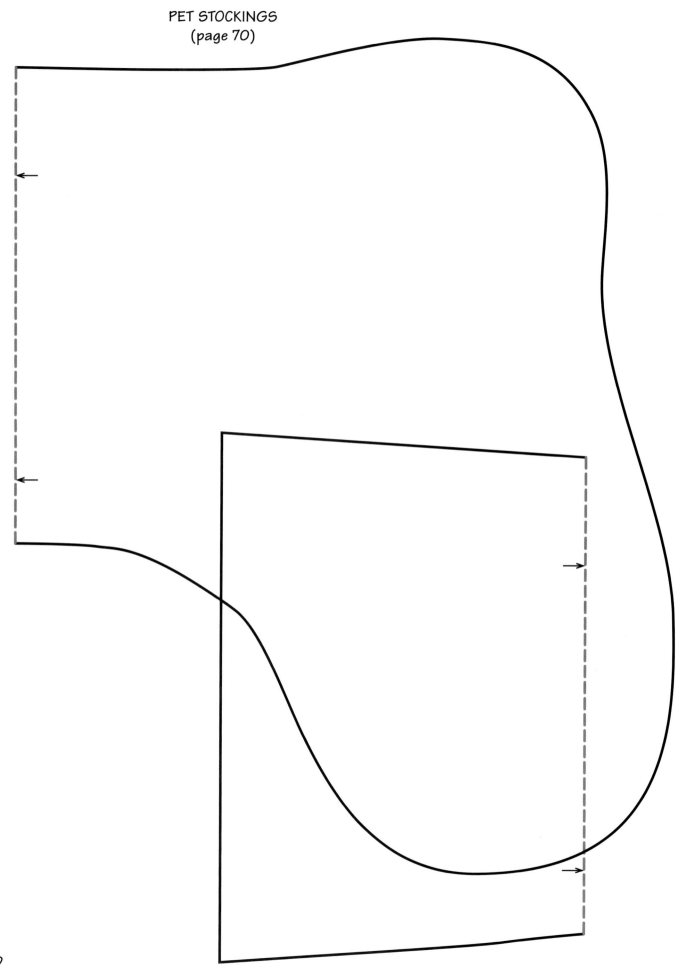

PET STOCKINGS
(page 70)

153

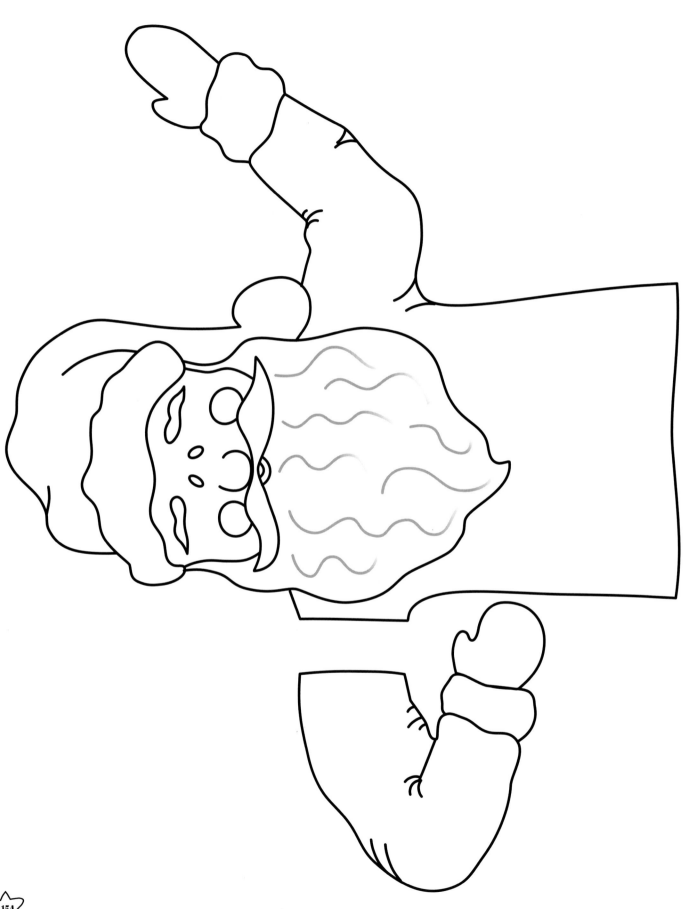

SAVORY BUTTERS BASKET
(page 79)

Savory Peppercorn Butter

Savory Parsley Butter

Savory fines herbes Butter

ONION SOUP MIX BAG
(page 81)

~ Onion Dip ~

Blend 5 tablespoons mix with 2 cups sour cream. Stir well and refrigerate at least 2 hours. Stir again before serving with fresh vegetables or potato chips.

~ Onion Soup ~

Combine 4 cups water with 5 tablespoons soup mix; bring to a boil. Simmer, uncovered, for 10 minutes.

~ Roasted Potatoes ~

Toss 5 tablespoons soup mix with peeled and cubed potatoes and 1/3 cup olive oil. Spoon on a 15" x 10" baking sheet and bake at 450 degrees for 35 to 45 minutes or until potatoes are tender

ANGEL GIFT TAG
(page 76)

to

ORIENTAL SAUCE BOTTLE
(page 78)

HOLLY'S
ORIENTAL STIR-FRY SAUCE

STORE SAUCE IN REFRIGERATOR UP TO 1 MONTH. SHAKE WELL BEFORE USING.

1 LB. MEAT
3 C. ASSORTED VEGGIES
1½ C. STIR-FRY SAUCE
2 T. OIL

IN LARGE SKILLET OR WOK, IN 1 T. OIL, STIR-FRY MEAT 'TIL NO LONGER PINK. REMOVE FROM PAN ~ SET ASIDE. STIR-FRY VEGGIES IN THE REMAINING OIL 2-3 MINUTES. ADD MEAT & STIR-FRY SAUCE. COOK AN ADDITIONAL 5-10 MINUTES. (MARINATE MEAT IN ¼ C. OF SAUCE BEFORE STIR-FRYING FOR MORE FLAVOR.)

SEWING GIFT BASKET
(pages 56-57)

I'm "SEW" glad we're Friends!

GIFT FILLED MILK BOTTLES
(page 58)

You're Sweet!

GARDEN GIFT POT
(page 59)
Enlarge pattern 150%

I have friends in overalls whose friendship I would not swap for the favor of the kings of the world.
—THOMAS EDISON—

PROJECT INDEX

RECIPE INDEX

Friends
are
the
sunshine of life.
- JOHN HAY -

Credits

We want to extend a warm *thank you* to the people who allowed us to photograph some of our projects at their homes: Carl and Monte Brunck, Nancy Gunn Porter and Cathy Swann.

We want to especially thank photographers Ken West of The Peerless Group, Little Rock, Arkansas, and Jerry R. Davis of Jerry Davis Photography, Little Rock, Arkansas, for their excellent work. Photography stylists Sondra Harrison Daniel, Karen Smart Hall and Charlisa Erwin Parker also deserve a special mention for the high quality of their collaboration with the photographers.

We extend a special word of thanks to Deborah Lambein, who designed the *Cross-Stitched Sampler* and *Mini-Sampler Ornament* shown on pages 31 and 32.

The pans used to bake the *Checkerboard Cake* shown on the front cover (recipe on page 102) can be purchased from Gooseberry Patch® product catalog, which is filled with cookbooks, cookie cutters, snowmen, angels, Santas and hundreds of other country collectibles. For a two-year subscription to "A Country Store in Your Mailbox®" send $3.00 to Gooseberry Patch, 600 London Road, Delaware, Ohio 43015.

We would like to recognize Viking Husqvarna Sewing Machine Company of Cleveland, Ohio, for providing the sewing machines used to make many of our projects, and Design Master Color Tool, Inc., of Boulder, Colorado, for providing the wood-tone spray used on several of our projects.

A special word of thanks to Rose Glass Klein, who made the *Cookie Pull Toys* shown on pages 48-49, and to Helen Stanton, who made the *Cross-Stitched Sampler* and *Mini-Sampler Ornament* shown on pages 31 and 32.